Sower's Seeds Aplenty
Fourth Planting

by

Brian Cavanaugh, T.O.R.

D0971787

Paulist Press
New York ☙ Mahwah, N.J.

Also by Brian Cavanaugh, T.O.R.
Published by Paulist Press

THE SOWER'S SEEDS
MORE SOWER'S SEEDS: SECOND PLANTING
FRESH PACKET OF SOWER'S SEEDS: THIRD PLANTING

Cover design by Fran Balles Goodman

Copyright © 1996 by Brian Cavanaugh, T.O.R.

Library of Congress Cataloging-in-Publication Data

Cavanaugh, Brian, 1947-
    Sower's seeds aplenty: fourth planting/by Brian Cavanaugh.
        p.   cm.
    Includes bibliographical references and index.
    ISBN 0-8091-3629-5 (alk. paper)
    1. Homiletical illustrations.   2. Catholic preaching.   I. Title.
BV4225.2.C35   1996
251'.08—dc20   95-51015
                                                                CIP

Published by Paulist Press
997 Macarthur Boulevard
Mahwah, NJ 07430

Printed and bound in the
United States of America

Contents

Dedication

I am dedicating this book to my mother, Julia Fenelon Cavanaugh, who instilled in me at a young age the excitement and adventure that can be discovered through reading. Growing up I cannot remember when there was not a book on the kitchen table near her coffee cup. My mother's example implanted in me a love to read books, all kinds of books. And I want to take this moment to thank her.

And, by the way, a thank you to my mother for insisting on bringing "the little guy" back for the cover of *Fresh Packet of Sower's Seeds: Third Planting*. It seems "the little guy" has become a mascot for what is becoming *The Sower's Seeds Series*.

Acknowledgments

Again, I am so grateful to all the people who have purchased my first three books—*The Sower's Seeds, More Sower's Seeds: Second Planting* and *Fresh Packet of Sower's Seeds: Third Planting*. Your letters of interest and encouragement certainly support my feelings that we are a people of stories. Stories and storytelling form the core of our values and beliefs.

I sincerely acknowledge the contributions of Donna Menis in editing the initial draft and providing valuable insights and suggestions. Also I want to acknowledge Maria Maggi, my editor at Paulist Press, for her encouragement, prodding, tweaking over the last few months.

A Creed for the Sowing of Seeds

"A man throws seed on the land. Night and day, while he sleeps, when he is awake, the seed is sprouting and growing; how, he does not know."

Mark 4:26–28

I believe that this is one of the earth's finest moments, that the sun lifting yellows and greens into life of tiny poplar leaves is much like God's own Spirit of love lifting life into me.

I believe that the Word of God has many times been planted in my life, often because of another who received the seed in ready soil, brought forth a harvest, and shared that goodness with me.

I believe that the call to be a sower of the Word is a privilege and a blessing, that no one can ever earn the right to claim the duty, that it is a gift freely given and a ministry to be constantly celebrated in gratitude.

I believe that great things can come forth from even the tiniest seed planted in love and cared for tenderly in the heart of another.

I believe that usually only God knows what sprouting and greening will come from the Word planted through my ministry. I am content in knowing that I have tried, with the Sower's grace, to seed that Word in faith and with joy.

I believe that even the most insignificant aspects of life can be the seed of God's gifting, that deeper faith can root and mature in very ordinary soil.

I believe that some dying of seed has to take place before it can give itself over to life, that every heart has its germination time, its dark moment, before the future hallowedness of harvest comes.

I believe that it takes much patience to sow a seed, to freely give it away to the heart of the earth, to allow it to take root and to grow in its own good time.

I believe that my life will always know its season of hope, that I will find flowers after every finality of ice and snow, that I will find green, growing things after every harsh, barren reign of winter's rage.

and most of all...

I believe in the Sower of all seeds, in the God of Springtime, in the Giver of all good and growing things, my Lord and my God!

Preface

As an avid collector, compiler and publisher of inspirational, motivational and uplifting stories, I was delighted when I first discovered Father Brian Cavanaugh's *Sower's Seeds* books. I was unable to put them down—finishing each volume in a single sitting. As I read each book I earmarked some pages, put Post-it Notes® on others, and made marginal notes on still others. I immediately thought of specific uses for almost every story—to make points in my lectures and seminars on self-esteem and peak performance, as an illustration in a point I wanted to make to one of my three sons, and for possible inclusion in the many books I was working on.

Father Cavanaugh has drawn these wonderful stories from many, many traditions, cultures and spiritual paths, but all have the power to make important points for our lives today. He has sifted through hundreds of books, articles, and newsletters to find these timeless golden nuggets hidden among the thousands of illustrations authors and teachers have used down through the ages and into the present time to stimulate our thinking, awaken our hearts and guide our behavior. He has saved us readers thousands of hours of prospecting and led us directly to the mother lode of wisdom and inspiration.

As I had the pleasure to read this new volume, I was struck by the variety of entries—beautiful and moving poetry, inspirational and uplifting stories, powerful reflections on age-old questions, important insights into our daily challenges, challenging questions to ponder and an occasional joke to get us to laugh at ourselves. All in all we are left with a deeper sense of what is important, a clearer sense of our spiritual work, and a more profound sense of the essence of life's journey.

We are lucky to still have storytellers and story collectors in America. The storytellers have an important role to play in our lives. They wake us up to who we really are. They remind us of something deeper in us that seeks expression in our daily lives. When we become numb to our stories, we lose touch with the core of our being. All the great teachers throughout human history have known the power of stories. Jesus taught in parables. The Buddha told stories to illuminate his teachings. The Sufi masters of the middle east have told stories for centuries to awaken the mind of the listener to a higher order of knowledge. And our most effective elementary and high school teachers, our best coaches and our favorite college professors used both true stories and mythic tales to capture our attention and lock their messages forever into our memories.

Father Brian Cavanaugh has given us a treasure chest full of some of the best teaching stories ever compiled in this new collection which he has entitled *Sower's Seeds Aplenty*. Whether you are a teacher looking for illustrations for your lectures, a minister seeking stories to use in your sermons, or simply a person seeking to further your own personal and spiritual growth, you will find what you are seeking in this magnificent book.

Now let me make a recommendation here. It comes from my twenty years' experience of using stories to teach and to transform. While it would be easy to sit and read this entire book in one reading—as I have often been tempted to do because the stories are short and so very entertaining to read—I am going to advise you not to gulp this book down in one sitting. Instead, I advise you to take your time and to read each story as if it contained a very valuable treasure that can only be discovered by slow and careful examination. Father Cavanaugh gave us an important clue to this when he named these tales *Sower's Seeds*. Indeed, a seed must be carefully planted, watered and tended to until it can grow into a fully mature plant. Likewise, each of these stories contains a seed of greater wisdom, a seed of higher consciousness and a seed of greater insight into the truth of life. You must let these seeds germinate and grow inside you to get their full value.

If you try to assimilate all of these stories in one reading, you run the risk of suffering from spiritual indigestion. You can only fully integrate true wisdom into your life in small, bite-sized doses. To truly "get" each story you need to stop after reading it and ask yourself the following questions: How does this story relate to me and my life? What can I do *today* to apply what I have learned here? What specific behavior or behaviors can I engage in with my family, with my friends, at work and at church to demonstrate my understanding and application of this new insight? How can I share this insight with my family, friends and co-workers?

When you have answered these questions and put the answers into practice, then let yourself go on to the next story. Only then will you get the full value that is possible from this magnificent book.

If you are a teacher, preacher, minister, priest or parent, make sure that you ask yourself these same questions before you attempt to use these stories in your teaching of others. It's the old dictum of walking your talk before you talk it. There are two reasons for this. The first is that you will get to experience the benefits of all this applied wisdom in your own life. The second is that when you tell these stories, they will have a greater chance of "ringing true" in the mind of the listener because there will be integrity and congruence in your speaking.

Having stated these caveats, let me now invite you to begin this magical journey of reading, perceiving, delighting in and living the higher truths contained in this wonderful new collection of *Sower's Seeds.* Enjoy!

Jack Canfield
Co-author, *Chicken Soup for the Soul*

1.
Granny's Glasses

Walter Buchanan

A little boy said to his playmate, "When I get older, I want to wear glasses just like Granny's because she can see so much more than most people. She can see the good in a person when everyone else sees a bad side. She can see what a person meant to do even if he or she didn't do it. I asked her one day how she could see the good, and she said it was the way she learned to look at things as she got older. And when I get older, I want a pair of glasses just like Granny's so I can see the good, too."

How different our world would be if we all wore a pair of Granny's glasses! If I would look for the good in you, and you would look for the good in me, our lives would be so much more pleasant. At times, we are like the buzzard that seeks out what is rotten and ugly, when we should be like the hummingbird that looks for what is sweet and beautiful. I dare you to try on a pair of Granny's glasses!

2.
"When Will I Die?"

Anonymous

In 1910 a newspaper column carried the following story: Jimmy, age ten, was a devoted brother to his sister, age six. He nearly panicked when his sister fell off her bicycle and cut a large artery in her leg. The bleeding was profuse, and by the time a doctor arrived at the scene, the little girl was close to dying.

Now, in the early 1900s blood transfusions were not yet common practice. Carrying the girl into the house, the doctor managed to clamp the cut ends of the artery, but the little girl's heart was still failing. In desperation, the doctor turned to Jimmy and asked, "Jimmy, will you give some of your blood to help save your little sister's life?"

Jimmy swallowed hard, but nodded his head. So the doctor placed him on the kitchen table and began withdrawing blood from one of his veins. Then he injected the blood directly into the little girl's vein.

For the next thirty minutes, the doctor and the family anxiously watched over the little girl and prayed. The doctor kept his stethoscope over her heart to note its beating. Finally, she was over the crisis. The doctor wiped the perspiration off his brow. Only then did he notice that Jimmy was still stretched out on the kitchen table, tense and trembling. "What's the matter, Jimmy?" asked the doctor. "Wh-wh-when will I die?" replied Jimmy through clenched teeth.

The doctor realized that Jimmy misunderstood what the request for his blood really meant. Jimmy imagined that his sister was going to need all his blood, which meant that Jimmy, though hesitating a moment and swallowing hard at the doctor's original request, silently had agreed to die for his little sister!

The doctor had tears in his eyes as he reassured Jimmy that he had extracted only a little of his blood for his sister, and that Jimmy was not going to die. Jimmy was willing to sacrifice, even his life, so that his sister might live.

3.
Worry Chokes Opportunity

Anonymous

It is significant that the English word *worry* is derived from an Anglo-Saxon word, *worien*, that means "to strangle"

2

or "to choke." Worry cuts off the air supply that allows one to *carpe diem* (Latin for *seize the moment*).

People get so busy worrying about yesterday or tomorrow that they miss today. We become like the old woman who said, "I always feel bad when I feel good, because I just know that I'll feel bad after a while."

Worry chokes off the opportunity to seize the moment and makes us susceptible to a life of feeling bad.

4.
Satan's Beatitudes

Anonymous

Blessed are they who are too tired and busy to go to church on Sunday, for they are my best workers.
Blessed are they who are bored with the minister's mannerisms and mistakes, for they get nothing out of the sermon.
Blessed are they who gossip, for they cause strife and divisions that please me.
Blessed are they who are easily offended, for they soon get angry and quit.
Blessed are they who do not give their offerings to carry on God's work, for they are my best helpers.
Blessed are they who profess to love God but hate their own brother or sister, for they will be with me forever.
Blessed are the troublemakers, for they shall be called the children of the devil.
Blessed is he or she who has no time to pray, for that person shall be easy prey.

5.
Transformation Through Encouragement

Anonymous

A businessman in a hurry plunked down a dollar into the cup of a man selling flowers and rapidly went his way. Half a block down the street, he turned around and made his way back to the poor flower seller. "I'm sorry," he said picking out his favorite flower. "In my haste I failed to make my purchase. After all, you are a businessman just like myself. Your flowers are fairly priced and of good quality. I trust you won't be upset with my forgetting to pick out my purchase." With that he smiled and quickly went on his way again.

A few weeks later, while at lunch, a neatly dressed, handsome man approached the businessman's table and introduced himself. "I'm sure you don't remember me, and I don't even know your name, but your face I will never forget. You are the man who inspired me to make something of myself. I was a vagrant selling flowers on a street corner until you gave me back my self-respect and a sense of dignity. Now I believe I am a businessman, too."

6.
Good Tidings of Great Joy!

Anonymous

In western Canada a young missionary told the native tribes of the love of God. To the Indians it was like a revelation. After the missionary had spoken, an old chief asked, "When you spoke of the Great Spirit just now, did I hear you say, 'Our Father'?"

"Yes," said the missionary.

"That is very new and sweet to me," said the chief. "We never thought of the Great Spirit as Father. We hear him in the thunder; we see him in the lightning, the tempest and the blizzard, and we were afraid. So when you tell us that the Great Spirit is *our father,* that is very beautiful to us." The old man paused, and then he went on, as a glimpse of glory suddenly shone on him. "Missionary, did you say that the Great Spirit is *your* Father?"

"Yes," replied the missionary.

"And," questioned the chief, "did you say that he is the *Indians'* Father?"

"That I did," said the missionary.

"Then," exclaimed the old chief, like a man on whom a dawn of joy had burst forth, "*you and I are brothers!*"

7.
Believe—Behave

Anonymous

The old country preacher used to say: "There are two parts of the gospel. The first is the believing part, and the second is the behaving part."

8.
Big Feet—Bigger Heart

Anonymous

It was an unseasonably hot day. Everybody, it seemed, was looking for some kind of relief, so an ice cream store was a natural place to stop.

A little girl, clutching her money tightly, came into the store. Before she could say a word, the store clerk sharply told her to get outside and read the sign on the door, and stay out until she put on some shoes. She left slowly, and a big man followed her out of the store.

He watched as she stood in front of the store and read the sign: **No Bare Feet.** Tears started to roll down her cheeks as she turned and started to walk away. Just then the big man called to her. Sitting down on the curb, he took off his size 12 shoes, and set them in front of the girl, saying, "Here. You won't be able to walk in these, but if you sort of slide along, you can get your ice cream cone."

Then he lifted the little girl up, and set her feet into the shoes. "Take your time," he said. "I get tired of moving them around, and it'll feel good to just sit here and eat my ice cream." The shining eyes of the little girl could not be missed as she shuffled up to the counter and ordered her ice cream cone.

He was a *big* man, all right. Big belly, big shoes, but, most of all, he had a *big heart*.

9.
The Berry Spoon

Anonymous

"I'll never forgive him. I told him I would *never* forgive him."

The elderly lady spoke softly, but with resolve, as the nurse brought her her nightly medication. The lady's expression was troubled as she turned away, focusing on the drape wrapped around her nursing home bed. This brief exchange revealed a deep, deep hurt.

She told of how her brother had approached her bed, accusing her of taking more than her share of family heirlooms following their mother's death. He spoke of various items, ending with "the berry spoon." He said, "I want the berry spoon." For the forty years since the mother's death he had hidden his feelings, and now they erupted.

She was both hurt and angered by his accusation and vowed never to forgive him. "It's my spoon. Mother gave it to me," she defended herself. "He's wrong and I won't forgive him."

Standing at her bedside, the nurse felt her own spirit soften and grieve. A spoon—a berry spoon! In the bed lay a woman given two months to live—just sixty days—and she would face eternity and never see her brother again in this

6

life. Her mind and spirit were in anguish, and her only remaining family ties were broken over a berry spoon.

As the nurse returned to her station she was drawn deep into thought: "How many berry spoons are there in my life? How many things, as insignificant as a spoon, in light of eternity, separate me from God—and from others? How does a lack of forgiveness keep me separated from my family?" She asked God to search her heart. "How many berry spoons are there in my life?"

10.
Dogs & Christians

Roy Osborne

A woman recounted an interesting occurrence: "There was a terrible racket outside, and when I went to the window I saw a large dog standing just outside the fence, and my dog was angrily barking at it. Have you ever noticed that the dog inside always barks angrily at the dog outside, but the dog outside does not bark at all? Well, that's the way it works with dogs, I reckon."

She continued, "I recognized the dog outside as belonging to a neighbor, and I knew the dog should not be running loose. So I opened the gate and let it into the yard with my dog. The barking stopped. A bit of sniffing took place while the two dogs made sure of each other, and then they both proceeded to ignore each other. Both dogs ignored each other completely. But that's the way it is with dogs!"

The woman went on reflectively, "It occurred to me that that is the way with church members also. The ones outside never bark, but the ones inside often bark angrily at those not on the inside with them. However, once they come inside, and after we make sure of them, we proceed to completely ignore them unless they happen to be in our social crowd."

She thought, "It would be nice if we changed the rules

and stopped acting like dogs! Wouldn't it be better if we would extend our hands and be friendly to those outside our group? Wouldn't it be so much better if we did not ignore one another, except for an occasional sniff and a handshake at church or during a holiday?"

Just how many broken hearts might be mended, how many tears dried if we cared enough to notice and to share a bit of genuine love. There has been much written of pets being brought into rest homes to cheer up those who are lonely. It is too bad that a puppy with a wagging tail can bring more comfort and acceptance than we do. But, after all, that's the way it is with dogs. How about with you?

11.
Kill the Spider

Anonymous

There was a man who faithfully attended a weekly prayer meeting, always confessing the same thing during testimony time. His prayer seldom varied:

O Lord, since we last gathered together, the cobwebs have come between you and us. Clear away the cobwebs, Lord, that we may again see your face.

At a later meeting, another person called out shortly after the man had started his weekly litany, "O Lord God, kill the spider!"

12.
Don't Ignore Jesus

Anonymous

I'm sure you are familiar with the expression, *Kids say the darndest things*, or maybe the adage, *Out of the mouths of babes . . .*

As the story goes there was an inquisitive four-year-old who happened to be rooted strongly in the "Why" and "Tell me" stage of life. The boy was helping his father set up the Christmas decorations. Imagine the scene with boxes scattered about, and listen to the conversation:

"Daddy, why are there so many lights? What do all these colors mean? Why do you cut branches off the tree and hang them on the door? Did you help your daddy when you were big like me? Tell me again the story of baby Jesus. Why do we bring a tree in the house? Mommy's going to get mad if you make a mess."

Does that sound familiar? Well, it continues. The little boy was helping to sort out ornaments and said, "Daddy, what does *ignore* mean?"

The father explained, "Ignore means not to pay attention to people when they call you."

Immediately the little boy looked up at his father and said, "I don't think we should ignore Jesus."

Puzzled, the father knelt closer to his animated son and replied, "I don't think we should ignore Jesus either, son. I think we should give him our full attention. Why do you say that we ignore him?"

"But, Daddy, that's what the Christmas carol says, "Oh come let us ignore him."

Kids sure do say the darndest things, don't they? But, you know, often we actually get so caught up in the frenzy of preparations, parties, shopping and decorating that we appear to ignore the true meaning of Christmas, and fail to prepare a place in our hearts to come and adore him.

13.
The Living Dead!

Dr. Ashley Montagu

Dr. Ashley Montagu, the outstanding anthropologist, spoke at the University of Miami. He stayed at a hotel on famed Fort Lauderdale beach. While being chauffeured along the fabulous Gold Coast en route to the university, he observed the people along the streets and on the beaches. Traveling down a main street, Dr. Montagu turned to his student escort and exclaimed, "Look, the living dead!"

The student, somewhat puzzled by the comment, asked Professor Montagu what he meant. He replied, "I see people here trying so hard to have a good time, but they have a *hollow* look about them, they appear *empty* behind the eyes. Many of them live so superficially. I can't think of any way to describe them but as the *living dead*."

14.
Rule of Life?

Anonymous

A major league baseball owner once spoke of the "Zeke Bonura Rule of Life." You see, old Zeke was a crummy first baseman, and one of the game's worst fielders. Yet every year he would end up with the best fielding percentage in the major leagues.

Now Zeke was no braintrust, but he knew better than anyone that you could never get charged for an error if you didn't touch the ball. So with this in mind, he managed to avoid anything that looked remotely difficult.

Does this rule rule your life?

15.
On Setting Standards

Alan Loy McGinnis

A highly regarded music teacher, when asked about her unusual success with students, said, "First, I teach them that it is better to do it well than to do it badly. I guess that may seem quite rudimentary, but it is surprising how many students have never been taught the pleasure and pride in setting standards and then living up to them."

16.
Get People To Sign

Anonymous

One Sunday a visiting businessman went to church, and after the service congratulated the minister on his sermon. But he added a bit of constructive criticism.

"If you were one of my salespeople, I'd have a talk with you. Your appearance and your voice got my attention. Your delivery aroused my interest. What you said needed to be said. It made a lot of common sense. But then you stopped. You didn't go on to ask me to do something about it. In business, you have to get people to sign on the dotted line; otherwise, you'll soon be out of business."

17.
Noah's Ark Football

Anonymous

Time was passing slowly on Noah's ark, so the tiger suggested to the giraffe that they choose sides for a football game. All the animals agreed. The tiger's team kicked off, and on the first play the monkey handed off to the rhino who ran up the middle for a touchdown. Then the rhino ran it in for the two extra points. Every time the giraffe's team got the ball, they handed off to the rhino who ran for one touchdown after another. At halftime, the giraffe's team was ahead 84–0.

In the second half, the monkey again handed off to the

rhino. The rhino headed toward the line, but the centipede, playing defensive tackle, tripped the rhino with its many feet. The rhino fell to the ground and fumbled the ball. The rabbit, playing free safety, scooped up the ball and ran for a touchdown. The crowd went wild.

The tiger was elated. "Fantastic tackle!" he exclaimed to the centipede. "But where were you during the first half?"

The centipede replied, "Hey, I was lacing my shoes."

18.
Turn Fear and Worries Over to God

Anonymous

Babe Ruth is one of the most colorful players baseball has ever known. He is also one of the most famous names in American sports. One cold December night in 1946, the words of Jesus—*Repent, for the kingdom of heaven is at hand*—took on special meaning for the Babe. He explained why in an article: "Even though I drifted away from the church, I did have my own altar, a big window in my New York apartment overlooking the city lights.

"Often I would kneel before that window and say my prayers. I would feel quite humble then. I'd ask God to help me . . . and pray that I'd measure up to what he expected of me."

On this cold December night, however, the Babe was lying in bed in a New York hospital, seriously ill. Paul Carey, one of Babe's oldest and closest friends, was at his side. After a while, Carey turned to Ruth and asked, "Babe, they're going to operate in the morning. Don't you think you should see a priest?"

Ruth saw the concern in Carey's eyes, and for the first time in his life he realized that death could *strike him out*. The kingdom of heaven was, perhaps, at hand for him. He knew he had to take seriously Jesus' words: *Repent, for the kingdom of heaven is at hand.* Ruth looked into Carey's eyes and said, "Yes, Paul! I'd appreciate your calling a priest."

That night Babe Ruth spent a long time talking to Jesus with the priest's assistance. When he finished, Babe had made a full and humble confession. He didn't hold back on a thing.
"After the priest left," the Babe said, "and I lay in bed that evening, I thought what a comfortable feeling to be free from fear and worries. I could simply turn them over to God."

19.
"The Still"

Anonymous

When disaster strikes on a British naval vessel, a signal called "The Still" is sounded. This signal means:
"Stop what you're doing. Pause. Check your situation. Prepare to do the wise thing."
Before the signal is sounded, few sailors know what is the wise thing to do. During the pause they learn what it is.
We too run into emergencies in daily life. We too don't know what to do immediately. We cry out, "What can we do?" Actually, the best thing we can do is to pause and be still.
Pausing often spells the difference between success and failure.

20.
Repent—Not Do Penance

Anonymous

A pastor was conducting a Vacation Bible Study class on the New Testament. He discovered a word which was translated *do penance,* whereas another version rendered the same word as *repent*. He asked the children if they knew the difference between penance and repentance.

A short silence was broken by a girl who asked, "Is it not this? Judas did penance and went and hanged himself, while Peter repented and wept bitterly."

The doing of penance is external action, while repentance goes to the heart of the matter.

21.
Desire To Excel

Anonymous

Charles Schwab, former president of U.S. Steel, had a mill manager whose men were not producing their quota of work. "How is it," Schwab asked, "that a man as capable as you cannot make this shift turn out its quota?"

"I don't know," the manager replied. "I have coaxed the men, pushed them, but nothing seems to work. They just will not produce."

It happened to be the end of the shift, just before the night shift came on. "Give me a piece of chalk," Schwab said. Then, turning to the nearest worker, he inquired, "How many turns of the furnace did your shift produce today?"

"Six," he said.

Without another word Schwab chalked a big figure 6 on the floor, and he walked away.

When the night shift came in, they saw the big 6 and asked what it meant. "The boss was here today," the day shift said. "He asked us how many turns we made, and chalked it on the floor."

The night crew grumbled among themselves, "Those lazy louts on the day shift. Six turns of the furnace? We'll show them!"

The next morning Schwab walked through the mill again and noticed that the night shift had rubbed out the 6 and replaced it with a big 7. The day shift couldn't believe those buffoons from the night shift could work that much. So they went about production determined to show the night shift that their work was not that remarkable. When the day shift went home that night they left behind an impressive *10*. Shortly, the mill which had been lagging way behind in production was turning out more work than any other company plant.

Without yelling a word or making any threats Schwab had made his point. He said, "The way to get things done is to stimulate competition. I don't mean in a sordid, money-getting way, but in the desire to excel."

22.
Family Is a Garden

Brian Cavanaugh, T.O.R.

Celebrating the feast of the Holy Family is a time to look at Joseph, Mary and Jesus as a R.E.A.L.* family, an earthly family, not a pious, out-of-this-world type of family. They are a family that understands the great anxieties and sorrows of family life. The Holy Family is our model of how a family can be holy and R.E.A.L. By R.E.A.L. I mean **Respecting–Encouraging–Affirming–Loving.**

It's been said that the family is a garden and that whatever is planted in it will grow. Planting these four values in your family will bring forth a harvest of an abundant family life. I am reminded also that there exists the Law of the Fallow Field. Simply stated, this law holds that if nothing positive is planted in the garden, it will always revert to weeds. Yes, we have to continually plant each growing season exactly what it is we expect to grow; if nothing of value is planted, nothing of value will be harvested.

---

* Inspired by Eugene Wallace

So here are some suggestions for your family garden:

A family, like a garden, needs . . .
* time, attention and cultivation.
* sunshine of laughter and affirmation.
* the rains of difficulties, tense moments of anxieties and serious discussions on important matters.
* areas of hardness to be turned over, i.e., bitterness, envy, anger, unforgiven hurts.

In this family garden, plan to plant seventeen rows . . .
* 5 rows of P's: Perseverance, Politeness, Praise, Peace-making and Prayer.
* 4 rows of "let us": Let us be faithful in word and deed, Let us be unselfish with our resources, Let us be loyal, Let us love one another.
* 3 rows of squash: Squash gossip, Squash criticism and Squash indifference.
* 5 rows of "turn ups": Turn up on time for school plays, scout meetings and baseball games, Turn up for family gatherings, Turn up with a better attitude, Turn up with new ideas and the determination to carry them out, and Turn up with a smile.

If you plant and nurture these "value seeds" in your family garden, you will bring to a bountiful harvest a R.E.A.L. family, as well as a holy family.

23.
Joining—Participating

Anonymous

Someone once called a pastor to say he wanted to join the parish. He went on to explain, however, that he did not want to have to go to Mass every Sunday, study the bible, be a lector or an usher, visit the sick, or help out with C.C.D. classes.

The pastor commended him for his desire to be a member of the parish, but told him that the church he wanted was located across town. The man took the directions and hung up.

When he arrived at the address the pastor gave him, he came face to face with the logical consequence of his own apathetic attitude. For there stood an abandoned church and several other buildings, all boarded up and ready for demolition.

24.
The Onion

Fydor Dostoevski

Once upon a time there was a peasant woman, and a very wicked woman she was. One day she died leaving not a single good deed behind. The devils caught hold of her and plunged her into the Lake of Hades.

Her guardian angel stood by and wondered what good deed of hers he could remember to tell God about. The angel mentioned, "Why, she once pulled up an onion from her garden and gave it to a beggar woman."

And God replied, "You take that onion then, hold it out to her in the lake, and let her take hold of it and be pulled out by it. If you can pull her out of the Lake of Hades, let her come into paradise. But if the onion breaks, then the woman must stay where she is."

The angel ran to the woman and held out the onion toward her. "Come and catch hold," cried the angel. "I'll pull you out." And he began cautiously pulling her out. He had almost pulled her out when the other sinners in the lake, seeing how she was being saved, began clutching hold of her legs so they, too, could be pulled out.

However, she was a very wicked woman and began kicking at them. "I'm to be pulled out, not you. It's my onion, not yours. Let go." As soon as she uttered these words, the onion broke. The woman fell back into the Lake of Hades where she remains to this day.

And the guardian angel wept as he went away.

25.
Let the Other Do It!

Anonymous

Four brothers decided to have a party to celebrate a new business venture. Since wine is rather expensive, they agreed that each one would bring an equal quantity and mix it together in a large serving bowl.

One of the brothers thought he might escape making his contribution by bringing water instead of wine. "It won't be noticed in the common bowl," he reasoned. But when, at the party, the wine was poured out, it turned out not to be wine at all but plain water. All four brothers had thought alike—cheap. Each one had thought, "Let the other do it!"

26.
The Working Person's Beatitudes

Mary Margaret Sekerak

1. Blessed are they who resist accepting promotions with strings attached, for their integrity and conscience shall be clear.
2. Blessed are reformed type-A's, for their efforts to change lifestyles shall be reflected in their physical and mental well-being.
3. Blessed are they with empathetic hearts and caring na-

tures, for they have not allowed life to make them callous and unconcerned.

4. Blessed are they who stop running after "the latest," "the newest," or "the most-improved," for they shall no longer be breathless and frustrated.

5. Blessed are they who refuse to play power games, for by resisting to do whatever it takes to get to the top, they will not leave a path of broken lives and bruised spirits.

6. Blessed are the spontaneous, for they have learned how to laugh and enjoy the present.

7. Blessed are they who are willing and comfortable to admit they are wrong, or—better yet—admit they are imperfect, for they will be considered really human.

8. Blessed are they who do not get caught up in a "treadmill mentality," for they shall know the simple joys of smiling, hugging and simply being.

9. Blessed are they who can see the "big picture," for they will always have the vision to look beyond the here and now.

10. Blessed are the non-judgmental, who do not specialize in putting others down.

11. Blessed are they who stop to listen, for they shall discover that learning is endless and may come from unexpected sources.

12. Blessed are they who give of their time and of themselves, for their recipients will have been given two of the most valuable gifts on earth.

13. Blessed are former perfectionists, for they shall realize that they are allowed to make mistakes.

14. Blessed are struggling ex-workaholics, for their relationships and home lives will benefit from their revised priorities.

15. Blessed are they who, at some point, realize their total dependence on God and their inter-dependence on others, for in doing so, they will have discovered life's most valuable lessons.

27.
Witness of Faith

Anonymous

A teenage girl named Anne got a summer job working as a maid in a hotel at an oceanside resort. Her job was to clean ten rooms every day. In the course of the summer, Anne met all kinds of interesting people, including a few celebrities. Of all the people she met, however, one stood out from all the others. She called him Mr. Smith.

Mr. Smith showed up one weekend with only an overnight bag. When Anne went to clean his room, he stuck his head out of the door and said, "Forget about cleaning my room. Just give me a couple of clean towels." The next two days were exactly the same. It wasn't until mid-week that Mr. Smith allowed Anne to clean the room. As she did, he talked to her and even helped her make the bed.

On Saturday Anne cleaned her usual ten rooms, including Mr. Smith's room. After she finished, Anne was walking down the lane on her way to 4:30 Mass. Suddenly a car pulled up next to her. It was Mr. Smith. "Can I give you a ride?" he asked. She said she was going to church and would welcome a ride there.

Once Anne was inside the car, Mr. Smith asked her a barrage of questions: How often did she go to Mass? Why did she go when lots of teenagers didn't? How good were the sermons? Did she always receive communion?

"Come and see," replied Anne.

When they arrived at the church, Mr. Smith asked Anne if he could go to Mass with her. She began to feel a little wary about this stranger and his odd questions. But her feelings eased when Mr. Smith knelt down, shut his eyes and remained that way throughout the Mass.

At the end of Mass, Mr. Smith got up and hurried outside without even saying goodbye. The next day, when Anne went to clean his room, the travel bag was gone. In its place was a small box with a note attached. She unfolded the note and read it. The note read something like this:

"Dear Anne,

The gift inside the box is for the beautiful thing you've done for me without even knowing it. My marriage has been rather shaky lately—so much so that I finally told my wife that I was moving out for a few days to think things over. The more I thought, the more confused I got.

Then you came along. You invited me to 'come and see.' Your beautiful faith in God touched me deeply. When I attended Mass with you, it was for the first time in ten years. During that Mass God gave me an insight into my problems and the desire to stay with my wife.

I'm going home, grateful to God and grateful to you for being a shining light in a time when my world was very dark. I will never forget you for helping me rediscover my faith.

(signed) Mr. Smith."

Inside the box was a gold chain with a beautiful gold cross attached to it.

28.
Water on Stone

Abba Poemen

The nature of water is soft, that of stone is hard. But if a bottle is hung above the stone, allowing the water to fall— drop by drop—it wears away the stone.

So it is with the word of God, the bible. It is soft and our heart is hard. Yet the person who listens to the word of God allows the hardness of his or her heart to open up to the grace of God.

29.
Legend of the Dogwood

Anonymous

At the time of the crucifixion, the dogwood had reached the size of the mighty oak tree. So strong and firm was the wood that it was chosen as the timber for Jesus' cross.

To be used for such a cruel purpose greatly distressed the dogwood. While nailed upon it, Jesus sensed this, and in his compassion he said, "Because of your pity for my suffering, never again shall the dogwood tree grow large enough to be used for a cross. Henceforth, it shall be slender, bent, and twisted, and its blossoms shall be in the form of a cross—two long and two short petals.

"In the center of the outer edge of each petal will be the print of nails. In the center of the flower, stained with blood, will be a crown of thorns so that all who see it will remember."

30.
That Basic Truth

Ralph W. Sockman

A scoutmaster told his scouts to remember: "In the woods we are the guests of the animals and trees and plants." I like that!

A refined person is very careful of the house and furniture where he is being entertained. He handles objects there with even more care than if they were his own. Likewise, as guests of God, we are courtesy-bound to conserve the resources of God's good earth—its forests, its soil, its oil, its water—that we may leave for posterity a land richer than we found. We sometimes act as if our country's resources were inexhaustible and also wholly our own. Not so!

"The earth is the Lord's and everything in it" (1 Cor 10:26). Let us not forget that basic truth.

31.
Find Your Artichokes

Anonymous

Fr. Mark Link tells of when the musician Andre Kostelanetz once visited the French artist Henri Matisse. When Kostelanetz got to Matisse's home, his nerves were frayed and he was exhausted. Matisse noticed this and said to him goodhumoredly, "My friend, you must find the artichokes in your life." With that, Matisse took Kostelanetz outside to his garden.

When they came to a patch of artichokes, Matisse stopped. He told Kostelanetz that every morning, after he has worked for a while, he comes to this patch of artichokes to pause and be still. He just stands there looking at the artichokes.

Matisse added, "Though I have painted over 200 canvases, I always find new combinations of colors and fantastic patterns. No one is allowed to disturb me in this ritual. It gives me fresh inspiration, necessary relaxation, and a new perspective toward my work!"

Find the artichokes in your life!

32.
Wisdom or a Goat

Anonymous

The king of Spain once dispatched a youthful nobleman to a court of a neighboring king, who received the dignitary with the objection: "Does the king of Spain lack men, that he sends me a beardless boy?"

The youthful ambassador replied, "Sir, if my king had supposed you imputed wisdom to a beard, he would have sent you a goat."

33.
Purpose of Life

Anonymous

While on vacation a husband and wife team of psychologists lounged by the pool. Seemingly out of nowhere, a young girl appeared next to them. She told the couple her name was Jessica and that she was seven years old.

The husband had a habit of asking *to-the-point,* tough questions. He looked over at the bright-eyed girl and whimsically asked her, "What is life all about?"

Jessica thought for a second before replying. "The purpose of life is to be kind and loving," she said, "to be here for other people, to make the world a better place than before you came."

Bolting upright, the husband and wife asked the girl where she had learned these things. "Did you learn them from your parents?"

"No," Jessica answered.

"In school?"

"No."

"At church, then?"

"Uh, no."

"Well, where did you learn such things?" they asked the youngster.

"I just knew them before I came here," she said.

Looking back at our lives, remember how much we knew as children—how much we knew of truth and honesty. How much of that have we given up or forgotten? How much have we surrendered out of our own fears, surrendered in desperate need to fit into society, surrendered to compromise our integrity?

34.
Believe Without Understanding

Anonymous

A young college student, considered to be an intellectual elitist, announced to a group of friends that he would believe nothing that he could not understand. Another student, who lived on a farm nearby, turned to the intellectual and remarked, "As I drove to campus today, I passed a field in which some sheep were grazing. Do you believe it?"

"Sure," replied the young man.

"Well, not far from the sheep," the student-farmer said, "some calves were chewing on the fresh grass. Do you believe it?"

"Yeah, why not?"

"Well, not too far down the road there was a gaggle of geese feeding. Do you believe this?" asked the student-farmer.

"I guess so," came the reply.

"Well," said the student-farmer, "the grass that the sheep ate will turn into wool; the grass that the calves ate will turn into hair; the grass that the geese ate will turn into feathers. Do you believe this?"

"Sure I do," the too-smart student answered.

"But do you understand it?"

"Uh, no," the intellectual student said, somewhat puzzled.

"You know," said the student-farmer, "if you live long enough, you will find that there are a great many things you will believe without understanding."

35.
Test in Honesty

Anonymous

The professor told his class, "Today I'm giving two examinations—one in calculus and the other in honesty. I hope you will pass them both. But if you must fail one, then fail calculus. There are many good people in the world who cannot pass calc, but there are no good people in the world who cannot pass the test of honesty."

36.
Josh and His Jag

Josh Ridker

About ten years ago a young and very successful executive named Josh was traveling down a Chicago neighborhood street. He was traveling a bit fast in his sleek, black, 16 cylinder Jaguar XKE, which was only two months old.

He watched for kids darting out from between parked cars and slowed down when he spied legs between two cars. As his car passed the opening where the legs were, a brick sailed and—whump—smashed into the Jag's shiny side door.

SCREECH, brakes are slammed, gears are pounded into reverse, tires madly spin the Jaguar back to the spot from where the brick was thrown. Josh jumped out of the car, grabbed the kid and pushed him up against a parked car. He shouted at the kid, "Just what was that about? Who do you think you are?" Building up a head of steam he continued, "That's my new Jag; that brick is going to cost you plenty. Why did you throw it?"

"Please . . . please, mister, I'm sorry. I didn't know what else to do," pleaded the youngster. I threw the brick because no one else would stop."

Tears were dripping down the boy's chin as he pointed around the parked car. "It's my brother, mister," he said. "He fell out of his wheelchair and I can't lift him up." Sobbing the boy asked the executive, "Would you please help him back into his wheelchair? He's too heavy for me."

Stunned to the bone, the young man tried desperately to swallow the rapidly swelling lump in his throat. He helped the youngster upright the wheelchair, and the two of them lifted his brother back into the chair.

It was a long, long walk back to the sleek, shiny, black 16 cylinder Jaguar XKE—a long and slow walk. Now, Josh never did fix the side door of his Jaguar. It reminded him not to go through life so fast that someone has to throw a brick at him to get his attention.

37.
The Dismissal Rite

Mark Link, S.J.

A C.C.D. teacher asked students in her confirmation class which part of the liturgy, or Mass, was the most important part. She was not prepared for the answer from one of the students.

The youth said, "The dismissal rite is the most important part of the Mass."

"Why do you say that?" asked the teacher.

The teenager replied, "The purpose of the eucharist is to nourish us with the word of the Lord and the body and blood of the Lord, so that we may go forth to bear witness to the Lord and to bring the kingdom of God into existence."

The student continued, "The eucharist does not end with the dismissal rite. In a sense, it begins with it. We must go forth and proclaim to the world what the disciples of Emmaus did. We must proclaim that Jesus is risen. We must proclaim that Jesus lives on."

The youth was absolutely correct.

This is the message the world needs to hear. This is the message the world must hear. If we don't deliver this message to the world, we have failed in our mission as Jesus' disciples. In a very true sense, the dismissal rite is the most important part of the Mass.

38.
Live More Abundantly
(adapted)

William Arthur Ward

Shrimp wear their skeletons on the outside of their bodies, and have been known to discard their shells as many as twenty-six times during a lifetime. They shed their shells to accommodate their growing bodies.

Perhaps we human beings can take a lesson from the shrimp. Do we have some shells that need discarding? It may be a good idea to examine our lives and shed a few shells occasionally. The growing person is constantly shedding his or her shells.

The pessimist is limited by doubts, confined by fears, and restricted by uncertainties. The optimist is freed by faith, stimulated by hope, and encouraged by confidence.

Perhaps it's time to shed our shells of envy, pride, anger, indifference. What the world needs now is greater enthusiasm for life. Enthusiasm is the key that unlocks the doors to abundant life. Perhaps it's time to shed our shells of selfishness and of narrow, confining self-interest. The generous person is the joyous person. The giving spirit is the beautiful spirit. Follow the example of the Master Teacher and give generously, willingly, unhesitatingly, and completely.

39.
More Than Holy Words

Anonymous

There was a young monk who sat outside the monastery, his hands clasped in prayer. He looked very pious and chanted holy words all day. Day after day he intoned these words, believing that he was acquiring grace.

One day the head priest of the monastery sat next to him and began rubbing a piece of brick against a stone. Day after day he rubbed one against the other. This went on week after week, until the young monk could no longer contain his curiosity. He finally blurted out, "Father, what are you doing?"

"I'm trying to make a mirror, said the priest.

"But that's impossible!" said the monk. "You can't make a mirror from brick."

"True," replied the priest. "And it is just as impossible for you to acquire grace by doing nothing except chanting all day long."

40.
People Who Keep the World Running

Anonymous

A couple strolled about in New York City one warm evening. They came upon a ConEd electric generating station, quietly humming about its business. The wife mused, "Though we've lived nearby, we have never known it was here."

Some people are just like that—people who quietly do their jobs, run farms, fix shoes, pump gas, cut hair, and teach children. Like ConEd quietly keeps the city and its suburbs running, inconspicuous people like these keep the world running.

41.
Life Is an Empty Bottle

Anonymous

Earlier this century, a woman went to her doctor with a catalogue of complaints about her health. The physician examined her thoroughly and became convinced that there was nothing physically wrong with her. He suspected it was her negative outlook on life—her bitterness and resentment—that was the key to her feeling the way she did.

The wise physician took the woman into a back room in his office where he kept some of his medicine. He showed her a shelf filled with empty bottles. He said to her: "See those bottles? Notice that they are all empty. They are shaped differently from one another, but basically they are all alike. Most importantly, they have nothing in them. Now, I can take one of these bottles and fill it with poison—enough poison to kill a human being. Or I can fill it with enough medicine to bring down a fever, or ease a throbbing headache, or fight bacteria in one part of the body. The important thing is that I make the choice. I can fill it with whatever I choose."

The doctor looked her in the eye and said, "Each day that we are given is basically like one of these empty bottles. We can choose to fill it with love and life-affirming thoughts and attitudes, or we can fill it with destructive, poisonous thoughts. The choice is ours."

And what will you choose? Life-affirming, positive, healing thoughts? Or the seething poisons of anger, bitterness and prejudice? The choice is yours!

42.
The Great Guest in Rhyme

Anonymous

It happened one day at the year's white end—
Two neighbors called on their old-time friend;

And they found the shop, so meager and mean,
Made merry with a hundred boughs of green.
Conrad, the cobbler, was stitching, a face ashine,
But suddenly stopped as he twitched a twine;
"Old friends, good news! At dawn today,
As the roosters were scaring the night away,
The Lord appeared in a dream to me,
And said, 'I am coming your Guest to be!'
So I've been busy with feet astir
Strewing the floor with branches of fir.
The wall is washed and the shelf is shined,
And over the rafter the holly twined.
He comes today, and the table is spread
With milk and honey and wheaten bread."

His friends went home; and his face grew still
As he watched for the shadow across the sill.
He lived all the moments o'er and o'er,
When the Lord should enter the lowly door—
The knock, the call, the latch pulled up,
The lighted face, the offered cup.
He would wash the feet where the spikes had been,
He would kiss the hands where the nails went in,
And then at the last would sit with Him
And break the bread as the day grew dim.

While the cobbler mused, there passed his pane
A beggar drenched by the driving rain.
He called him in from the stony street
And gave him shoes for his bruised feet.
The beggar went and there came a crone,
Her face with wrinkles of sorrow sewn.
A bundle of coal bowed her back,
And she was spent with the wrench and rack.
He gave her his loaf and steadied her load
As she took her way on the weary road.
Then to his door came a little child,

Lost and afraid in the world so wild,
In the big, dark world. Catching her up
He gave her the milk in the waiting cup.
And led her home to her mother's arms,
Out of the reach of the world's alarms.

The day went down in the crimson west,
And with it the hope of the blessed Guest,
And Conrad sighed as the world turned gray:
"Why is it, Lord, that your feet delay?
Did you forget that this was the day?"
Then soft in the silence a voice he heard:
"Lift up your heart, for I kept my word.
Three times I came to your friendly door;
Three times my shadow was on your floor.
I was the beggar with bruised feet;
I was the old woman you gave food to eat;
I was the child on the nameless street."

43.
You Have a Special Message To Deliver

Anonymous

There is an old Jewish-Christian tradition which says:
God sends each person into this world
with a special message to deliver,
with a special song to sing for others,
with an act of love to bestow.

No one else can speak my message,
or sing my song, or offer my act of love.
These are entrusted only to me.
According to this tradition,
the message may be spoken,
the song sung, the act of love delivered

only to a few, or to all the folk in a small town,
or to all the people in a large city,
or even to all those in the whole world.

It all depends on God's unique plan for each person.
To which we might add:
The greatest gift of God, one would think,
is the gift of life.
The greatest sin of humans, it would seem,
would be to return that gift,
ungrateful and unopened.

44.
On the Wings of Success or Failure

Anonymous

Dr. Stephen Langley invented a heavier-than-air machine that had its first successful flight on May 6, 1896. Most people and a vast number of scientists remained skeptical of Dr. Langley's invention, especially after the first plane officially commissioned by the government (in 1898) met with an accident while launching on December 8, 1903. The machine failed to fly and fell into the Potomac River instead.

Langley, wounded by the scorn of other scientists and the criticism of the public, retrieved his heavier-than-air machine and stored it in a warehouse. He died of a broken heart on February 27, 1906. Only a few days after Langley's unsuccessful attempt of flight, on December 17, 1903, Wilbur Wright made the first successful flight in the Wright brothers' airplane.

Interestingly, in 1914 the old Langley machine was taken from the Smithsonian Institution and with a Mr. Curtis in the pilot's seat, it was flown successfully over Lake Keuka. If only Dr. Langley had persevered in trying longer.

45.
On the Wrong Train

Warren Wiersbe

When a railway conductor began collecting tickets one morning, he discovered that the first passenger had the wrong ticket.

"I'm sorry, sir," said the conductor, "but you're on the wrong train. You will have to change trains at the next station."

He collected several more tickets and found that these passengers, too, were carrying the wrong tickets. It seemed strange that so many should have made the same mistake. Then he discovered the truth. He, the conductor, was on the wrong train!

46.
Two Golden Days

Robert J. Burdette

There are two golden days in the week about which I never worry—two carefree days kept sacredly free from fear and apprehension.

One of these days is yesterday. Yesterday, with all its cares and frets, all its pains and aches, all its faults, its mistakes, and blunders, has passed forever beyond recall. I cannot unsay a word once said. All that it holds of my life—of wrong, of regret and sorrow—is in the hands of the Mighty Love that can bring honey out of the rock and the sweetest water out of the bitterest desert. Save for the beautiful memories, sweet and tender, that linger like the perfume of roses in the heart of the day that is gone, I have nothing to do with yesterday. It was mine. It is God's now.

And the other day that I do not worry about is tomorrow. Tomorrow, with all its possible adversities, its perils, its large

34

promise and poor performance, its failures and mistakes, is as far beyond my mastery as its dead sister, yesterday. It's God's day. Its sun will rise in splendor or behind a mass of clouds, but it will rise.

Until then, the same love and patience that held yesterday, holds tomorrow. Save for the star of hope and faith that gleams forever on the brow of tomorrow, shining with tender promise into the heart of today, I have no possession in that unborn day of grace. Tomorrow is God's day. It will be mine.

There is left for myself, then, but one day in the week—today! And you can fight the battles of today. Any person can resist temptation for just one day. Any man or woman can carry the burdens for just one day. It is only when we willfully add the burdens of those awful eternities, yesterday and tomorrow—such burdens as only the mighty God can sustain—that we break down. It isn't the experience of today that drives people mad, it is the remorse of something that happened yesterday, and the dread of what tomorrow brings. Those are God's days; leave them with God.

Therefore, I think and I do and I journey, but one day at a time. That is my day. Dutifully, I run my course and work my appointed task on that day of mine; and God, the Almighty and All-loving, takes care of yesterday and tomorrow.

47.
What's Eating You?

Lewis Thomas

The Bay of Naples, Italy, is the habitat of a jellyfish called medusa and a snail of the nudibranch variety.

When the snail is small, the jellyfish will sometimes swallow it and draw it into its digestive tract. But the snail is protected by its shell and cannot be digested. The snail fastens itself to the inside of the jellyfish and slowly begins to eat it, from the inside out. By the time the snail is fully grown, it has consumed the entire jellyfish. If this was a crime it would be what is called an "inside job."

Many of us are like the jellyfish, and have our own snail that eats at us from the inside. Our snail may be alcohol, anger, insecurity, depression, worry, greed, etc. Slowly, it grows and begins to gnaw at us. We seethe internally, and eventually we are consumed from the inside.

So what's eating you?

48.
"Loafs" and Fishes

Anonymous

The Sunday school teacher asked her class, "Which parable in the bible do you like the best?"

One child quickly piped up, "The one about the loafs and the fishes."

49.
Gloomy Gus

W.A.M. Stover

Gloomy Gus was not his name, but that is what we called him, behind his back and sometimes to his face. "GG" was pessimism personified, a disciple of perpetual gloom. GG was a pessimist who liked to listen to the patter of little defeats. To be around GG was terribly depressing. He was a defeatist. Everything was wrong. The whole world was bad and getting worse. GG always felt unjustly abused, maligned and unlucky. He was full of self-pity, bitterness and resentment.

To GG everything was the darkest shade of black. There was no white or gray. GG looked at a bleak world through dark glasses. Each morning he arrived at the office in a gloomy mood to match his black hat, black tie and black suit. He seldom arrived without his black umbrella, for he constantly expected it to rain all over him. He had the whole wide world on his back, couldn't forget it, and wouldn't let you forget it either.

Why do people like Gus always look for the worst? Why do they forget that we can only go into the woods halfway, and the rest of the time we're coming out?

50.
Rating Code for Sermons

Anonymous

"G"—Generally acceptable to everyone. Full of inoffensive, puerile platitudes; usually described as "wonderful" or "marvelous."

"PG"—For more mature congregations. At times this sermon makes the Gospel relevant to today's issues; may even contain mild suggestions for change. Often described as "challenging," though no one intends to take any action or change any attitudes.

"R"—Definitely restricted to those not upset by truth. This sermon "tells it like it is." Threatening the comfortable; most often described as "disturbing" or "controversial"; usually indicates that the preacher has an outside source of income.

"X"—Positively limited to those who can handle bombshell-explosive ideas. This sermon really "socks it to them." It is the kind of sermon that landed Jeremiah in the well, got Amos run out of town, surprised Jonah, nailed Jesus to the Cross, set things up for the stoning of Stephen; always described as "shocking" or "in poor taste." The minister who preaches this sermon had better have his/her suitcase packed and life insurance paid in full.

51.
Supermarket Sweepstakes

Anonymous

Once there was a supermarket sweepstakes in which the five finalists were each given a fifteen minute shopping spree. Whoever accumulated the highest total on the register receipt would be declared the winner.

The finalists sped through the aisles, scooped up expensive items, crashed carts into one another, and bounced off store fixtures. It was a hectic, mad-dash race among the contestants.

From around an aisle there appeared a young man who sauntered along, casually selected items off the shelf and placed them in his cart. Amid the pushing and shoving, one of the finalists gaped at him as he slowly moved along. She shouted to him, "Why are you poking along and not in a hurry like everyone else?"

"Me?" he replied. "Why my father owns the store."

For many people, life is approached as if it were a sweepstakes game, with everyone running and bumping into one another. They are consumed with greed to accumulate the most things. We need to learn from Jesus that there is more to life than a mad-dash race. He reminds us that God is our Father, and, after all, he owns the store.

52.
A Penance To Remember

Ronald Mohnickey, T.O.R.

There was a woman who continually stood up waving her arms during the celebration of the Mass, as if in ecstasy. She rebuffed every attempt by the ushers to quiet her down and became agitated if they came too close to her. This went on week after week.

Finally the pastor approached her after Mass, whispered something in her ear, and she immediately snapped her hands to her side. From that day on she never again stood up during the Mass waving her arms.

A couple of weeks later one of the ushers congratulated the monsignor for quieting her down and asked him what it was that he had said to her. The pastor said with a twinkle, "Why, I told her that standing up and waving your arms is the penance I give for adultery!"

53.
A Royal Decree

Anonymous

A long, long time ago a beloved king died. The king's son, the queen and the rest of the immediate royal family were deeply saddened. For days after the king's death, they gathered at the prince's estate to console one another and finalize the funeral arrangements. They could not bear to enter the king's castle, such was the extent of their grief.

During this time, many relatives from near and far gathered at the prince's estate. There was a multitude of relatives. The prince, touched by the outpouring of sympathy, welcomed them all. The prince's wife and family offered great hospitality to the guests. Food and wine were abundant. Everyone had his or her fill.

The multitude of visitors put a tremendous strain on the prince's household. Tending to the needs of so many was difficult. But the prince, his wife and family—without complaint—pitched in behind the scenes with ordinary household chores to see to it that their guests were comfortable. They did this while mourning the late king.

As was the local custom, a lavish funeral was planned.

Such an event was terribly strenuous for the royal family because persons from far and wide would be there to pay their final respects. Also, as was the custom, a great feast was planned to mark the king's passing into heaven.

With the hour growing late on the night before the funeral, the revelry continued. The weary prince approached the gathered multitudes and, begging their understanding, asked them to return to their homes. He explained a time was needed for quiet contemplation and rest, especially by the queen, because the coming day would be so arduous on her. And the guests departed.

The next day, the king was laid to rest with all the pomp and ceremony befitting great kings. Immediately afterward, the prince once again threw open his estate and invited all the guests to return for a great feast and hearty celebration.

A few years later, the guests were invited to return to the castle to celebrate the birth of the new king's first son. Many returned and celebrated warmly. Recalling the night the prince asked them to return to their homes, a handful of others chose to stay away, saying, "We will not return to the castle because the prince once rudely cast us out."

When the prince first heard of this he was angered and hurt by such a rebuff. So, too, was the rest of the royal family. But when the anger subsided, a serenity of mind came upon them. They realized it is impossible to please everyone in life, and a time comes when there is no longer any need to try.

And so a decree went forth titled "Bad, Odd and Offensive Relatives." It stated that the royal family need never again feel obliged to invite this handful back to the castle. Naturally, the decree became known as the "B.O.O.R." decree, and through the years the insensitive louts at whom it was directed became known as boors.

The new king's family lived happily ever after.

The moral of the story, of course, is that you should always try to be a prince of a guy, but you don't have to let the boors get you down.

54.
More to Life

Grant Teaff

Coach Grant Teaff, in his book *I Believe,* describes an incident that happened early in his career at McMurray College. One Saturday night he and his team had just taken off in a chartered plane for the return to Texas. Suddenly the plane developed serious engine problems. The pilot announced that he would have to attempt an emergency landing. The plane was loaded with fuel, so an explosion also was likely.

As the plane sped downward, one of the players called out, "Coach Teaff, would you lead us in prayer? We're all pretty frightened." Teaff prayed out loud so everyone could hear.

Seconds later, the plane bellied across the runway. A shower of sparks engulfed the plane. Miraculously, however, it did not explode, and no one was hurt.

The next night Teaff and his family were in church together. Right in the middle of the service, Teaff got up, left the church, and went to the McMurray Fieldhouse about a mile away. He went straight to the team's dressing room and knelt down and prayed:

God, I know that you have a plan, a purpose, and a will for my life and the lives of these young men. I do not know what it is, but I'll try to impress upon the young men I coach this year and forever that there is more to life than just playing football, that you do have a purpose for our lives.

41

55.
Happiness Will Follow

Anonymous

There was an old alley cat watching a young kitten chasing its tail, round and round. The old cat ambled up to the kitten and asked, "Tell me, what are you doing?"

The kitten replied, "I just finished Cat Philosophy School. In my studies I discovered that in the world there are two things important for a cat. First, that happiness is the most important thing for a cat. Second, that happiness is located in one's tail.

"So what I've figured out is that if I chase it until I've finally got a hold on it, and get it in my mouth, then I'll have eternal happiness."

The old cat mused, "You know I'm just an alley cat. I haven't had the opportunity to go to the prestigious Cat Philosophy School like you. I've just wandered around alleys, here and there, all my life. But you know, it's amazing, I've kind of learned the same things you have. I've learned that the most important thing for a cat is happiness and, indeed, happiness is located in my tail.

"The only difference between you and me is that I've discovered that if you go about your business and do the things that are important to you, happiness will follow wherever you go."

56.
The Humble Thornbush

Anonymous

An unbeliever once asked the rabbi, "Why, of all things, did God choose the humble thornbush as the place from which to speak with Moses?"

The rabbi replied, "If God had chosen a carob tree or a mulberry bush, you would have asked me the same question. Yet it is impossible to let you go away empty-handed. That is why I am telling you that God chose the humble thornbush to teach that there is no place on earth bereft of the divine presence, not even a thornbush."

And this story finds its retelling in the story of Calvary. Calvary's tree is Moses' thornbush.

57.
The Station

Robert J. Hastings

Tucked away in our subconscious is an idyllic vision. We see ourselves on a long trip that spans the continent. We are traveling by train. From out of the windows we drink in the passing scene of children waving from a crossing, of cattle grazing on a distant hillside, of row upon row of corn and wheat, of flatlands and valleys, of mountains and hillsides, of city skylines and village halls.

But uppermost in our minds is the final destination. On a certain day at a certain hour, we will pull into the station. Bands will be playing and flags waving. Once we get there so many wonderful dreams will come true, and the pieces of our lives will fit together like a completed jigsaw puzzle. Now, restlessly, we pace along the train's aisles, waiting, waiting, waiting for the station.

When we reach the station, that will be it! But where is this station? When we buy a new 450SL Mercedes? When we put the last of the children through college? When we get *that* promotion? When we reach the age of retirement, shall we live happily ever after?

Sooner or later we must realize there is no single station, no one place to arrive at once and for all. The true joy of life

is the trip. The station is only a dream. It constantly outdis-
tances us.

Relish the moment is a good motto, especially when cou-
pled with Psalm 118:24—"This is the day which the Lord
has made; we will rejoice and be glad in it." It isn't the burdens
of today that drive men and women mad. It is the regrets over
yesterday and the fear of tomorrow. Regret and fear are twin
thieves which rob us of today.

So, stop pacing the aisles and counting the miles. Instead,
climb more mountains, eat more ice cream, go barefoot more
often, watch more sunsets, laugh more. Life must be lived as
we go along. The station will come soon enough.

58.
The Island Shell
(adapted)

Anne Morrow Lindbergh

Picking up a lovely shell from an early morning tidal pool,
the young woman said, "I shall name you *Island Shell*. I cannot
live forever on my island, on a vacation. But I can take you
back to my desk in my office. You will sit there and fasten
upon me images and visions of the sea. You will help me think
of the island I lived on for a few weeks. You will say to me
solitude. You will remind me that I must try to be alone for
part of the year, even a week or a few days, and for part of
each day, even for an hour or a few minutes in order to keep
my core, my center, my island quality.

"You will remind me that unless I keep the island quality
intact somewhere within me, I will have little to give to my
friends or the world. You will remind me that I must relax,
be still, as is the axis of a wheel, in the midst of my activities.
I must be the pioneer in achieving this stillness, not only for
my own salvation, but for the salvation of family life, of society,
perhaps even of our civilization."

59.
The Power To Change

Dr. Maxwell Maltz

Psychiatrist Alfred Adler got off to a bad start in arithmetic, and his teacher became convinced that he was "dumb in mathematics." The teacher advised Adler's parents of this "fact," and told them not to expect too much of him. They, too, were convinced. Adler passively accepted the evaluation they had placed upon him. And his grades in arithmetic proved they had been correct.

One day, however, he had a sudden flash of insight and thought he saw how to work out a problem which the teacher had put on the board, and which none of the other pupils could solve. He announced as much to the teacher. She and the whole class laughed.

Whereupon, Adler became indignant, strode to the blackboard, and worked out the problem, much to everyone's amazement. In doing so, he realized that he could understand arithmetic. He felt a new confidence in his ability, and went on to become a good math student.

60.
If You Won't, Who Will?

The Christophers

Professor Abraham Maslow used to challenge his students with questions like: "Which of you is going to write the next novel?" and "Who is going to be a saint like Schweitzer?"

Confronted with such big ideas, the students would only blush, squirm and giggle. Then the famed psychologist would assure them that he meant what he said. "If not you, who will?" he demanded. We could each ask that question of ourselves.

Each moment, God holds out a chance for us to be more, to achieve more. Each moment, God gives us what we need to respond to that invitation. We have what it takes. Will we use it? If not us, who will?

61.
The Servant of the Kingdom

French Fable

There's a French fable that tells of how one day the king's trusted personal servant went walking in a dense part of the forest near the palace. There he stumbled while stepping over a log and fell down a hill. Brushing off the leaves and debris, he looked down and saw at his feet the proverbial magic lantern, which he promptly rubbed, releasing a genie.

The genie said, "Your finding this lantern was no accident. You've worked hard all your life. Now you may receive one wish. But make it carefully because you can have only one wish.

The servant replied, "All my life I've been in positions requiring that I serve others. In fact, I'm known as 'The Servant of the Kingdom.' In the future, I want people to wait on me, and I want servants to do everything for me."

Sure enough, when the man returned to the castle, the door was opened for him. His food was cooked, meals served, dishes washed and clothes cared for by others. He was not allowed to perform his usual work—everything was done *for* him.

For the first month, the newness of the experience amused him. The second month it became irritating. During the third month, it became unbearable. So the man returned to the forest and searched until he found the lantern, rubbed it, and the genie appeared again. The man said, "I've discovered that having people wait on me isn't as pleasant as I'd thought. I'd like to return to my original station in life and, once again, be 'The Servant of the Kingdom.'"

The genie replied, "I'm sorry, but I can't help you. I had the power to grant you only one wish."

The man said, "But you don't understand. I want to serve other people. I found it far more rewarding to do things for others than to have all those things done for me."

The genie just shook his head.

The man begged, "Please, you must help me! I'd rather be in hell than unable to serve others."

The genie said sorrowfully, "Oh, and where do you think you have been, my friend, for the last ninety days?"

62.
Inventive Success

Thomas Alva Edison

Thomas Alva Edison's life was filled with purpose. When he spoke about his achievement and success, he said, "The most important factors of invention can be described in a few words:

1. They must consist of definite knowledge as to what one wishes to achieve.
2. One must fix one's mind on that purpose with persistence and begin searching for that which one seeks.
3. One must keep on searching, no matter how many times one may meet with disappointment.
4. One must refuse to be influenced by the fact that somebody else may have tried the same idea without success.
5. One must keep oneself sold on the idea that the solution of the problem exists somewhere and that he will find it."

63.
The Unbreakable Chain

Anonymous

According to the tale, there was a famous blacksmith from ancient times who, having been taken prisoner and locked in a dungeon, began to examine the chains which bound him in order to discover some flaw in the links that might make it possible to break them.

His hopes were dashed when he found from some identifying marks upon the chain that it was of his own craftsmanship. And it had always been his boast that no one could break a chain which he had forged.

Thus it is with a sinner. One's own hands have forged the chain that binds, a chain that no human hand can break.

64.
The Beautiful and Mystical River
(adapted)

Kenneth J. Willers

Once upon a time, there was a man who went on a journey in search of a beautiful and mystical river. When he found the river, he sat down next to it. He drank of it deeply; he bathed in it; he fished from it; he played in it—and he even nearly drowned in it. This man was filled with joy at just being near the river.

The man stayed many days and nights at the river, listening to its mystical teachings. Before he left, he took a picture of the river and then set off for home.

Upon his return, his family, friends and townspeople all noticed the joy this man now radiated. They asked him what had happened to him at the river. They asked him many questions about the river, and they wanted to know the mystical teachings he had learned there.

The man told them, "You must go for yourselves and experience the river. You must see, listen, touch, taste and smell the river for yourselves. I could never fully describe or hope to explain the beauty and mystery I experienced from the river. Words can never say it all. I urge you: Go! Experience the river yourselves."

Instead the people found the man's picture of the river, and they took it from him. They put the picture in a special frame of gold, built a large building and hung the picture on the wall so they could come and gaze at it for hours at a time.

Seeing what had happened, the man was saddened. He wished he had never taken that picture of the beautiful and mystical river.

65.
Maintain Integrity

Anonymous

A while back, there was a story about Reuben Gonzolas, who was in the final match of his first professional racquetball tournament. He was playing the perennial champion for his first shot at a victory on the pro circuit. At match point in the fifth and final game, Gonzolas made a super "kill shot" into the front corner to win the tournament. The referee called it good, and one of the lineman confirmed that the shot was a winner.

But after a moment's hesitation, Gonzolas turned and declared that his shot had skipped into the wall, hitting the floor first. As a result, the serve went to his opponent, who went on to win the match.

Reuben Gonzolas walked off the court; everyone was stunned. The next issue of a leading racquetball magazine featured Gonzolas on its cover. The lead editorial searched and questioned for an explanation for this first-ever occurrence on the professional racquetball circuit. Who could ever imagine it in any sport or endeavor? Here was a player with everything officially in his favor, with victory in his grasp, who disqualifies himself at matchpoint and loses.

When asked why he did it, Gonzolas replied, "It was the only thing I could do to maintain my integrity."

66.
You Knew What I Was

Iron Eyes Cody

Many years ago, Indian youths would go away in solitude on what is called a vision quest to prepare for manhood. One such youth hiked into a beautiful valley, green with trees and bright with flowers. There he fasted and prayed. But on the third day, as he looked up at the surrounding mountains, he noticed one tall rugged peak, capped with dazzling snow.

"I will test myself against that mountain," he pondered. He put on his buckskin shirt, threw his blanket over his shoulders and set off to climb the peak. When he reached the top, he gazed out from the rim of the world. He could see forever, and his heart swelled with pride. Then he heard a rustle of leaves at his feet, and, looking down, he saw a slithering snake. Before he could move, the snake spoke.

"I am about to die," whispered the snake. "It's too cold for me up here; I'm freezing. There's no food and I'm starving. Put me under your shirt where I'll be warm and take me down to the valley."

"No," said the youth. "I'm forewarned. I know your kind. You are a rattlesnake. If I pick you up, you will bite, and your bite will kill me."

"Not so," said the snake. "I will treat you differently. If you do this for me, you will be special to me, and I will not harm you."

The youth resisted a while, but this was a very persuasive snake with beautiful diamond markings. At last the youth tucked the snake under his shirt and carried it down to the valley. There he placed it gently on the grass. Suddenly, the snake coiled, rattled and struck, biting the youth on the leg.

"But you promised . . ." cried the youth.

"You knew what I was when you picked me up," said the snake as it slithered away.

Iron Eyes Cody says, "I tell that story especially to young people who might be tempted by drugs, alcohol, or other temptations. I want them to remember the words of the snake: *'You knew what I was when you picked me up.'*"

67.
The Harness-Maker's Son

Anonymous

It was 1818 in France, and Louis, a boy of nine, was sitting in his father's harness-making workshop. The boy loved to watch his father work the leather.

"Someday, father," said Louis, "I want to be a harness-maker, just like you."

"Why not start now?" said the father. He took a piece of leather and drew a design on it. "Now, my son," he said, "take the hole-punch and a hammer and follow this design, but be careful that you don't hit your hand."

Excited, the boy began to work, but when he hit the hole-punch, it flew out of his hand and pierced his eye! He lost sight in that eye immediately. Later, sight in the other eye failed. Louis was now totally blind.

A few weeks later, Louis was sitting in the family garden when a friend handed him a pine cone. As he ran his sensitive fingers over the cone, an idea came to him. He became enthusiastic and began to create an alphabet of raised dots on paper so that the blind could feel and interpret what was written.

Thus, Louis Braille opened up a whole new world for the blind—all because of an accident!

68.
For the Love of . . .

Anonymous

Abba Abraham was a holy man and great ascetic. He had eaten nothing but herbs and roots for fifty years. He lived simply and very austerely in total self-discipline. His younger brother died, leaving a daughter with no one to care for her. So Abba Abraham took in his niece and nourished and cherished her. Mary grew up to be beautiful, both in body and spirit. She followed Abraham, prayed with him, and was filled with grace.

One day a wandering tinker stopped at Abba Abraham's for a brief rest. He marveled at the girl's beauty. While taking advantage of the hospitality offered by Abba Abraham, who was out visiting other monks, he was overcome by lust and raped the poor girl.

She was so mortified and ashamed that she ran away from her uncle and fled to the city where, feeling so violated and disgraced, she became a prostitute. In vain did Abba Abraham look for his niece, until he heard, months later, that she could be found at a certain tavern.

Abba Abraham disguised himself as a military officer and went to the tavern. He ordered a bottle of wine and a platter of beef, eating to his heart's content and downing it all to the amazement of the onlookers. After he finished his dinner, he asked the tavern keeper for the "wench" named Mary. "I have come a long way for the love of Mary," he said.

She was brought to him, not recognizing this hard drinking soldier. He grabbed her, and she said with a wink, "And what do you want, old timer?"

He looked intently into her eyes and with compassion said, "I have come a long way for the love of Mary."

At the sound of his voice, she recognized her uncle and wept bitterly. Mary returned home with Abraham as his beloved niece. She became known as St. Mary the Harlot. Abba Abraham, who, remember, had not eaten meat in fifty years, did that night—"for love of Mary!" Such was the love he bore for her.

69.
Faith in Ability

Anonymous

According to legend, when Michelangelo started out, he was ignored by his own generation and disdained by art critics. But he had faith in his ability, and he decided to use subterfuge on his critics.

He knew they were fascinated when someone excavated an old ruin and dug up a supposedly priceless work of art. So he stained one of his works and buried it where an excavating party was sure to find it.

The critics were enraptured. They pronounced it a work of rare value. The cardinal of San Giorgio was so impressed that he paid a large sum for it. Then Michelangelo told them of his hoax. The art critics were stunned, but had no choice but to admit that he was an artistic genius. After that, Michelangelo was commissioned to do important works.

70.
Where Do Mermaids Stand?
(adapted)

attributed to Robert Fulgham

A young pastor, finding himself in charge of some very energetic children, hit upon a game called *Giants, Wizards and Dwarfs.* "You have to decide now," the pastor instructed, "which you are—a giant, a wizard or a dwarf."

At that, a small girl tugged at his pants and asked pointedly, "But where do the mermaids stand?"

The pastor told her there are no mermaids, and she chimed in, "Oh, yes there are. I'm a mermaid!"

Now this precocious little girl knew what she was, and she wasn't about to give up on either her identity or the game. She intended to take her place wherever mermaids fit into the scheme of things.

So, where do the mermaids stand? And how about all those who are different, those who do not fit into other people's boxes or pigeonholes?

Answer that question and you can build a school, a community, a nation.

As that very wise little mermaid exemplified, "Diversity, like anything worth having, requires effort." It requires effort to learn about and respect differences, to be compassionate with one another, to be tolerant, to cherish one's own identity, and to accept unconditionally the same in others.

71.
The Bag Ain't Full Yet

William Arthur Ward

Six months after the owner of a small crossroads store was appointed postmaster, not one piece of mail had left the village. When deeply concerned postal officials from Washington investigated, the local postmaster explained, "It's simple; the bag ain't full yet!"

Our bag doesn't have to be full for us to share some of our blessings with others. If your bag isn't full, that doesn't matter. Use what you have; share what has so generously been given to you. Enrich the lives of others with what you now have, and soon you will find your cup running over with joy!

72.
Strength Through Struggle

Dr. Myrle Swicegood

A young girl who was responsible for taking care of chickens frequently peeked into the nests to see if the new chicks had arrived.

One day she saw many downy, yellow chicks huddled under a mother hen, but there were two eggs not yet fully hatched. She could see the little bodies pulsing and struggling for freedom through the tiny holes pecked out of the shells. Impulsively she decided to help, and took one of the eggs, gently pulled it open and peeled away the shell to free the chick.

The next moment is frozen in her mind. As she finished the job, the baby chick gasped, struggled and stopped breathing. Sensing something dreadful had gone wrong, she ran for her mother.

Her mother's experienced eyes immediately read the story. She could have scolded or punished the girl, but she chose to teach her. The mother's caring words explained that each chick has to struggle to free itself. Through its own struggles, it became strong enough to live outside the shell.

Understanding the little girl's good intention and lack of knowledge, she said, "There are some things in life that other people just cannot do for you; you have to do them for yourself."

Now older and a mother herself, the former little girl with good intentions often recalls that event. "Often as I have longed to fix things for other persons," she says, "I remember that they just might have to do this for themselves, and I must allow them to struggle."

73.
Two Buckets at the Well

Anonymous

Two buckets met at the well. One of them looked morose. "What's the trouble?" asked the second bucket sympathetically.

"Oh!" replied the first, gloomy bucket, "I get so weary of being dragged to this well. No matter how full I am, I always come back here empty."

The second bucket laughed. "How curious!" the second bucket chuckled, "Why, I always come here empty and go away full. I'm sure if you started to think this way, you would feel much more cheerful."

74.
The Star

Anonymous

The day of the Christmas pageant finally arrived. My niece, Kaitlinn, was so excited about her part that I supposed she was to be one of the main characters, though she had not told me what her part was. The parents were all there, and one by one the children took their places. I could see the shepherds fidgeting in the corner of the stage meant to represent the fields for the sheep. Mary and Joseph stood solemnly behind the manger. In the back, three young Wise Men waited impatiently. At the edge of the stage, Kait sat quietly and confidently.

Then the teacher began: "A long time ago, Mary and Joseph had a baby and they named him Jesus." She continued, "And when Jesus was born, a bright star appeared over the stable."

At that cue, Kait got up, picked up a large tinfoil star,

walked behind Mary and Joseph and held the star up high for everyone to see.

When the teacher told about the shepherds coming to see the baby, the three young shepherds came forward, and Kait jiggled the star up and down excitedly to show them where to come. When the Wise Men responded to their cue, Kait went forward a little to meet them and to lead the way. Her face was as brilliant as the original star must have been.

The playlet ended, followed by refreshments. On the way home Kait said with great satisfaction, "I had the main part."

"You did?" I questioned, wondering why she thought that.

"Yes," she said, " 'cause I showed everybody how to find Jesus."

How true! To show others how to find Jesus, to be the light for their paths—that is the finest role we can play in life.

75.
The Christmas Shell
(adapted)

Gerald Horton Bath

A missionary was visiting several islands in the South Pacific before Christmas. He had been telling his native students how Christians, as an expression of their joy, gave one another presents on Christ's birthday.

On Christmas morning, one of the natives brought the missionary a seashell of lustrous beauty. When asked where he had discovered such an extraordinary shell, the native said he walked many miles to a certain bay—the location where such shells could be found.

"I think," exclaimed the missionary with gratitude, "it was wonderful of you to travel so far to get this lovely gift for me."

His eyes brightening, the native answered, "Long walk part of the gift!"

76.
The Village Storyteller

Anonymous

There's an anthropologist who regularly goes to a small village in western Africa. She pokes all about, sticking her nose into every nook and cranny. During one visit, she discovered a collection of television sets stacked four deep in a hut at the edge of the village. Now, this village had been given the wonderful gift of electricity just a few years earlier. And no doubt some wonderful manufacturer had presented the people with the essential TVs. The anthropologist was confused by the fact that they were not used, so she went to talk to the village chief.

She asked him, "Why don't your people use the television sets?"

The head man replied, "We have our storyteller."

The anthropologist probed further, "Maybe so, but the television has the capacity of thousands of stories."

"That's true," said the head man, "but our storyteller knows us."

77.
True Reform

Anonymous

One day St. Francis was speaking with a member of Assisi's nobility. The count was bewailing the chaos and scandals that crept into the world. "Your lordship need not grieve for these things," replied the saint, "for there is a remedy for these problems."

The count asked, "What remedy can there be for such evils?"

St. Francis said, "It's simple. You and I must first be what we ought to be; then we shall have brought about an inner healing. Let each one do the same and the reform will be effectual. The worst is that everyone talks of reforming others, without trying to correct one's own chaos and scandal. In this way evil remains as disorder everywhere."

78.
Fill the Tank First

Dr. E. Stanley Jones

A tourist group, traveling by bus, careened over one of the worst winding roads in the world. The bus driver had driven in the Alps only once before, and it happened that on that trip he had almost gone over one of those terrifying, precipitous cliffs. He was nervous; so before starting the next trip he went in front of the bus and stood with folded hands, saying his prayers to the machine.

That done, the trip started, but he had not gone far when the engine of the bus began to overheat. There was no water in the radiator! This was quickly fixed. But when the bus was still many miles from its destination, the machine stopped while going up a hill. There was no gas in the tank! There the passengers stayed until finally rescued.

The driver had said his prayers to the machine, but he put no water in the radiator and no gas in the tank.

79.
Forgiveness Begins New Life

Doris Donnelly

One day a seven year old boy was riding in the back seat of the family car. He was sitting between his older brother and sister. Their mother was driving.

On this day their mother was feeling especially distraught over having been recently abandoned by their father. Suddenly, in a fit of anger, she spun around and slapped the seven year old across the face. She yelled at the boy: "And you! I never wanted you. The only reason I had you was to keep your father. But then he left anyway. I hate you."

That scene branded itself on the boy's memory. Over the years his mother reinforced her feelings toward him by constantly finding fault with him. Years later that son was able to tell his counselor, "I can't tell you how many times in the last twenty-three years I relived that experience. Probably thousands."

He continued, "But recently I put myself in my mother's shoes. Here she was, a high school graduate with no skills, no job, no money and a family to support. I realized how lonely and depressed she must have felt.

"I thought of the anger and the pain that must have been there. And I thought of how much I reminded her of the failure of her young hopes. And so one day I decided to visit her and talk to her. I told her that I understood her feelings and that I loved her just the same.

"She broke down and we wept in each other's arms for what seemed to be hours. It was the beginning of a new life for me, for her—for both of us."

80.
The Root System Is Trust

Elaine M. Prevallet, S.L.

The tree can be an apt image of our spiritual life, our journey to God. Every growth upward and outward necessitates a deepening and widening of the roots. Some species of deciduous trees have one root, the tap root, which extends downward to stabilize the tree at the center and to reach the deepest source of water. The root system branches outward to provide balance and to draw nourishment from the soil. Since the work of setting the roots takes time and energy, these trees often grow slowly. But this slowly developed root system is what secures their endurance as sturdy, hardy trees. In our spiritual lives, the root system is trust.

81.
Two Paths of Life

Anonymous

There is a legend among Native Americans concerning the two paths of life. One path slopes gently down some low hills to the valley below. The legend says that this is a broad and easy path, but it leads into the desert where death waits.

The other path winds upward over a steep and rocky trail. It is filled with many difficulties, and only the strong can reach the heights of the mountain where the eagles soar.

Through this legend, Indian parents teach their children that the easy way is not the best way. Strong character is built by facing the obstacles and overcoming them, instead of trying to avoid difficulties by seeking a life of ease.

82.
War or Peace

Anonymous

The presidential seal of the United States shows an American eagle clutching arrows (the symbol of war) in one talon and an olive branch (the symbol of peace) in the other.

On earlier versions of the seal, the eagle is shown facing toward the arrows. When Harry Truman was president, he decreed that on all future versions of the seal the eagle should face not toward the arrows but toward the olive branch. He said he wanted to make it clear that the United States should be turned toward peace, not war.

What about your lives? In which direction are you pointed—toward peace, or war?

83.
Wings of a Dream

Anonymous

Itzhak Perlman is one of the greatest classical musicians today. As he tells it, before he was four years old two things happened to him which shaped his future. First, he was crippled by polio, and, second, he heard a recording of the famed violinist Jascha Heifetz.

Perlman explained that though polio took away his legs, Heifetz's music gave him wings. It gave him a dream that set Itzhak on the road to musical greatness.

As former president Woodrow Wilson said: "We grow great by dreams. All big men are dreamers. They see things in the soft haze of a spring day, or in the red fire on a long winter's evening. Some of us let these great dreams die, but others nourish and protect them through bad days till they bring them to the sunshine and light which comes always to those who sincerely hope that their dreams will come true."

Don't let anyone steal your dreams!

84.
On Reading the Bible

Anonymous

An old man came up to his pastor and said, "Pastor, I've just finished reading the entire bible for the fifth time in my life."

The pastor looked at the old man and said, "The important thing, Mr. Jones, is not how many times you've been through the bible, but how many times the bible has been through you."

85.
Where's Headquarters?

Anonymous

There's a story about President Lincoln and General Hooker, who replaced General Burnside as commander of the Union forces. Hooker set out at once to establish a reputation for himself as a general who took action. Accordingly, Hooker's first dispatch to the president bore the inscription: "Headquarters in the Saddle."

Lincoln noticed the heading on Hooker's dispatch but was not impressed. Said the president to an associate, "The trouble with Hooker is that he's got his headquarters where his hindquarters should be."

86.
Moses and Bush

Anonymous

President George Bush telephoned the Israeli prime minister Yitzhak Shamir one afternoon. Shamir was in a conference, so the president was placed on hold for a moment. When the prime minister got on the phone, President Bush let him know in no uncertain terms that he did not like to be kept waiting.

Shamir replied, "I'm sorry, Mr. President. I was meeting with someone more important."

"Just who is more important," Bush inquired, "than the President of the United States?"

Shamir said, "I was meeting with Moses. In fact, he's with me now."

"What?" Bush exclaimed. "You know Moses and he's with you now! Get him on the phone. I'd like to talk with him."

Shamir put the president on hold again as he talked with Moses. Quickly, he was back and said, "Moses doesn't want to talk with you. He said that the last time he talked to a bush it cost him forty years wandering in the wilderness."

87.
Are There Lawyers in Heaven?

Msgr. Arthur Tonne

Once the gate was knocked down separating heaven from hell. St. Peter appeared at the broken gate and called out to the devils gathering on the other side, "Hey, Satan, you're going to have to pay to get this fixed. Your devils knocked it down."

"No way," replied the chief devil. "My legions tell me they are not responsible."

"Well, then," grumbled St. Peter, "I'll file a lawsuit and sue you to repair the gate."

"Yeah, right," laughed Satan, "and where in heaven are you going to find a lawyer?"

88.
Do You Know Who I Am?

Anonymous

"I have never been guilty of wrong actions, but on my account lives have been lost, ships have been sunk, cities have burned, governments have failed, battles have been lost, and because of me a few churches have closed their doors.

"I have never struck a blow nor spoken an unkind word, but because of me homes have been broken, friendships have grown cold, laughter of children has ceased, wives have shed bitter tears, brothers and sisters have been forgotten and parents have gone brokenhearted to the grave.

"I have tended no evil, but because of me talents have come to naught, courtesy and kindness have failed and the promise of success as well as happiness has yielded sorrow and disaster.

"I have no sound, just silence. No cause for being myself. I have no offering to make except grief and sorrow. You may not in an instant call me by my name, but surely you are personally acquainted with me.

"My name? . . . **NEGLECT!**"

89.
Facing Rivers of Difficulties

Herb Smith

A very tired traveler came to the banks of a river. There was no bridge by which he could cross. It was winter, and the surface of the river was covered with ice. It was getting dark, and he wanted to reach the other side while there was enough light to see. He debated about whether or not the ice would bear his weight. Finally, after much hesitation and fear, he got down on his knees and began, very cautiously, to creep across the surface of the ice. He hoped that by distributing the weight of his body, the ice would be less apt to break under the load.

After he made his slow and painful journey about halfway across the river, he suddenly heard the sound of singing behind him. Out of the dusk there came a four-horse load of coal driven by a man singing merrily as he went his carefree way. Here was the traveler, fearfully inching his way on his hands and knees. And there, as if whisked along by the winter's wind, went the driver, his horses, his sled, and the heavy load of coal over the same river!

This story illustrates how so many of us go through life. Some stand on the banks of decisions unable to make up their minds about the course to take. Others stand on the banks trying to muster enough courage to cross over to the other side of the task or problem encountered. On the other hand, some individuals crawl and creep through life for fear of thin ice. Their faith is not strong enough to hold them up. Still there are those who whisk along whistling as they go. Their faith is unshakable.

When we face rivers of difficulties we do not have to fear, nor do we have to creep through life. God has promised to help, and with God's help we can merrily make our way to the other side, safely.

90.
Full-Time Occupation

Anonymous

A businessman was once asked, "What's your occupation?"

"I'm a Christian," was the reply.

"But what's your job?" asked the reporter.

The reply was the same: "I'm a Christian."

"You don't understand," pressed the reporter. "What do you do for a living?"

"Listen! My full-time job is to be a Christian; however, I own a furniture store to pay the bills."

91.
Good—Better—Best

Brian Cavanaugh, T.O.R.

Jesus said, "I came that they might have life and have it more abundantly" (Jn 10:10).

Why is it then that many individuals settle for less, or even least, in their own life? Did you ever hear a student ask, "Just tell me what I have to know for the test"? Or how about a person who inquires, "What's the minimum I need to do?"

To live abundantly parallels a marketing approach which features products as **good**, **better** or **best**.

It seems that most men and women, boys and girls, consider themselves to be good—at least good enough. Then there are other persons who believe that they are better than others—at least better than their peers. However, do these men and women ever discover their individual best, and do whatever needs to be done to abundantly live it out, whatever their personal best might be?

Abundant living does not settle for being simply better, or for being just good enough. It is to discover your best in every situation that you may have life and have it more abundantly.

92.
Dreams To Build On

Anonymous

Not that long ago a certain man used to drive his horse, Paddy, from store to store peddling his cheese products. As he did, he talked to Paddy about his dreams. But in spite of the long hours and hard work, the sales remained low and the debts rose.

One day a friend told him bluntly, "Lew, you're either too stubborn to admit it or too dumb to see it, but you're licked."

Lew Kraft refused to give up. He continued to visit stores peddling his cheese products and talk about his dreams to his horse, Paddy.

Today, the multimillion dollar Kraft Foods Company

stands as a testimony to a man who persevered in building on his dreams until they came true.

93.
Out of the Pit

Anonymous

A young man excitedly told his spiritual director about a dream he had the night before: "I dreamt I fell into a deep pit. Helpless and despairing I couldn't get out.

"A Confucist approached and said, 'Let me give you some advice, my friend; if you get out of trouble, never get in it again.'

"A Buddhist came and said, 'If you can climb up to where I can reach you, I will help you.'

"A Christian Scientist came along and said, 'You only think you're in a pit.'

"A self-righteous person said, 'Only bad people fall into pits.'

"A fundamentalist said, 'You must deserve your pit.'

"An I.R.S. agent asked, 'Are you paying taxes on this pit?'

"An optimist came along and said, 'Things could be worse.'

"A pessimist said, 'Things will get worse!'

"Then along came Jesus who, seeing my situation, jumped into the pit with me. He had me climb up on his shoulders and helped me out of the pit."

The young man discovered compassion was the greatness of being a Christian—to jump into the pit of life rather than standing on the sidelines as a spectator or an overseer.

And you, who call yourself a Christian, is there compassion like Jesus' in your life?

94.
How To Raise a Delinquent

J. Edgar Hoover

- You give him whatever he asks for, because it is easier than arguing.

- You pride yourself on not prying into her life—where she spends her time, her friends, her after-school activities.

- His side is your side in arguments with his teachers.

- Home is a battleground for her parents.

- You expect him to attend religious services but are too busy yourself.

- You say, "I'm busy now. Tell me later."

- She is expected to live up to the law, while you run through stop signs and cheat on your taxes.

- You smile when he scoffs at "squares" and admires those who "get away with it."

- You assume her problems are minor ones.

- White lies are all right for you, but he is expected to tell the truth, the whole truth.

- You think the world is against you, and you accept it.

- "Let George do it" is your attitude toward charity and community service.

- Your threatened punishments are not carried out.

- You are looking for "something for nothing."

- You never admit you could be wrong.

95.
Confidence and Teamwork

Anonymous

Sparky Anderson, the manager of the Detroit Tigers, makes the point that confidence is perhaps the most important part of playing good baseball. At the beginning of the 1989 season, when the Tigers were losing regularly, Anderson continually spoke of his confidence in the abilities of the players.

One day Sparky's team squeaked out a rare win. Analyzing the game, Sparky said, "Yesterday we got the confidence of about four of our players bolstered. Now if we can get the confidence of another four players bolstered tomorrow, we'll begin playing the way I know this team can play."

What a difference it makes when the leader has confidence in his players and will intercede on their behalf.

96.
A Grandfather's Prayer

Barry Lopez

One drizzly morning Barry got up and went off alone, before breakfast, for a walk in the woods. As he squished through the pines and cedars, he recalled a similar morning in his youth when he saw his grandfather go off alone through the same woods. When his grandfather returned, little Barry asked him where he had been and what he had done out there.

His grandfather smiled, put his arm around Barry and said, "Let's go get some breakfast."

As Barry continued his walk in the drizzle, he came to a clearing in the woods. There he knelt down and placed his hands flat against the damp earth. It gave him a feeling of being united with all creation. Barry recalled how his grandfather told him that if he ever felt lonely, he should go for a

70

walk in the woods, be quiet, and do whatever he felt moved
to do, like kneeling down and placing his hands flat against
the earth.

Half-an-hour later when Barry started back to the cabin,
he felt renewed. He felt recharged. Then he remembered why
his grandfather used to walk in the woods in the morning
twilight. Barry's grandmother once told him it was the way
his grandfather said his prayers. He would always end up on
the other side of the woods, standing on the beach with his
hands in his pockets, listening to the ocean.

97.
Gabriel's Secret Fear

Frederick Buechner

She struck the angel Gabriel as hardly old enough to have
a child at all, let alone this child, but he'd been entrusted with
a message to give her, and he gave it.

He told her what the child was to be named, and who
he was to be, and something about the mystery that was to
come upon her. "You must not be afraid, Mary," he said.

As he said it, he only hoped she wouldn't notice that
beneath the great, golden wings he himself was trembling with
fear to think that the whole future of creation hung now on
the answer of a young girl.

98.
Christmas Cookies

Pat Stackhouse

A mother related that Mr. Baker was a grouch. All the
neighborhood children said so. Her older boys used to fight
with his children—nothing serious, just bickering back and

forth. But Mr. Baker told a mutual friend that her children were brats and that he didn't like her family.

Along with her teenagers, the mother had a three year old son, Brian. For some reason Brian had always liked Mr. Baker, and even helped him work in his yard. He called him his "buddy." When Christmas rolled around, Brian wanted to bake some cookies and decorate them. "Mommy, I'd like to take a plate of my cookies to Mr. Baker."

She tried to discourage her son.

"Please, Mom," Brian pleaded. "We're pals."

And she gave in. It was Christmas, after all.

They put the cookies on a paper plate, covered them with foil, and placed a ribbon on top. She watched as Brian was greeted by Mr. Baker, who grinned as he took the cookies, dispelling her apprehension.

As he stood at the door, he yelled, "Merry Christmas," and waved.

"God bless you," she yelled back.

These were the first words spoken between the neighbors in seven years. Say, isn't that what Christmas is all about?

99.
Success Through Adversity

Anonymous

Three entrepreneurs parlayed a baffling setback into a major corporate success story. Early in their careers, during World War II, Ruth Handler, her husband Elliott, and their partner, Harold "Matt" Matson, designed plastic picture frames from scrap Lucite and scrap Plexiglas.

Ruth sold an order to a chain of photographic studios before her fledgling firm even had a shop. She was excited! As she drove downtown later to deliver the frames, an announcement came over the car radio: President Roosevelt had declared that all plastics, even scraps, were forbidden for any use other than defense. Reluctantly, Ruth turned the car around.

At this point, many entrepreneurs would have chucked the whole idea. But that night Ruth, Elliott and Matt discussed what to do. Elliott suggested that they make the frames out of wood and spray the wood to give it a cloth-look covering.

The next day Ruth found someone to cut the frames. When they were ready, she returned with them to the owner of the photographic studios and told the store owner she couldn't sell her plastic frames. The owner had heard the President's proclamation. Then Ruth held her breath and showed the owner the wooden frames. The woman was so pleased she gave Ruth an even larger order! That order gave Ruth, Elliott and Matt the confidence to rent a small shop for their picture-frame business.

Later on, with some slats of wood left over from making the frames, Elliott proposed they make dollhouse furniture. He sketched them out, Matt made the samples, and Ruth went out and sold them. That venture launched a company whose name is a combination of its founders, "Matt" and "Elliott"—*Mattel Toy Company.*

100.
In God's Time

Anonymous

Imagine a conversation with God. One day a man asked, "God, how long is a thousand years to you?"

The Eternal One answered with nary a blink, "Just a second."

"Well, then, Almighty," the man queried, "how much is a million dollars to you?"

The Creator of all shrugged it off with, "Just a penny."

With an idea in mind, a gleam in his eyes, and a flickering

smile crawling across his face, the man asked one more question, "Lord, can I have . . . well, uh . . . how about giving me just a penny?"

To which the Most High All-knowing replied with a slight grin, "Maybe . . . in just a second."

Source Acknowledgments

This book is the fruition of years of reading, listening and transcribing stories from many and varied sources. I thank the authors and publishers who have given their generous cooperation and permission to include these stories in this collection. Further reproduction without permission is prohibited.

Every effort has been made to acknowledge the proper source for each story; regrettably, I am unable to give proper credit to every story. When the proper source becomes known, proper credit will be given in future editions of this book.

GRANNY'S GLASSES
    Walter Buchanan
    Pulpit Helps, Vol. 14, #2
    PO Box 22000, Chattanooga, TN 37422–2000
    Used with permission

"WHEN WILL I DIE?"
    Anonymous
    Source Unknown

WORRY CHOKES OPPORTUNITY
    Anonymous
    Source Unknown

SATAN'S BEATITUDES
    Anonymous
    Pulpit Helps, August 1988, p. 11
    PO Box 22000, Chattanooga, TN 37422–2000
    Used with permission

TRANSFORMATION THROUGH ENCOURAGEMENT
  Anonymous
  Source Unknown

GOOD TIDINGS OF GREAT JOY!
  Anonymous
  Source Unknown

BELIEVE—BEHAVE
  Anonymous
  Source Unknown

BIG FEET—BIGGER HEART
  Anonymous
  Source Unknown

THE BERRY SPOON
  Anonymous
  Source Unknown

DOGS & CHRISTIANS
  Roy Osborne
  Source Unknown

KILL THE SPIDER
  Anonymous
  Source Unknown

DON'T IGNORE JESUS
  Anonymous
  Source Unknown

THE LIVING DEAD!
  Dr. Ashley Montagu
  Source Unknown

RULE OF LIFE?
Anonymous
Source Unknown

ON SETTING STANDARDS
Alan Loy McGinnis
Source Unknown

GET PEOPLE TO SIGN
Anonymous
Source Unknown

NOAH'S ARK FOOTBALL
Anonymous
Source Unknown

TURN FEAR AND WORRIES OVER TO GOD
Anonymous
Source Unknown

"THE STILL"
Anonymous
Source Unknown

REPENT—NOT DO PENANCE
Anonymous
Pulpit Helps, August 1990
PO Box 22000, Chattanooga, TN 37422–2000
Used with permission

DESIRE TO EXCEL
Anonymous
Source Unknown

FAMILY IS A GARDEN
Brian Cavanaugh, T.O.R.
Feast of Holy Family homily, December 1994

JOINING—PARTICIPATING
  Anonymous
  Source Unknown

THE ONION
  Fydor Dostoevski
  Source Unknown

LET THE OTHER DO IT!
  Anonymous
  Source Unknown

THE WORKING PERSON'S BEATITUDES
  Mary Margaret Sekerak
  Reprinted with permission

WITNESS OF FAITH
  Anonymous
  Source Unknown

WATER ON STONE
  Abba Poemen
  Source Unknown

LEGEND OF THE DOGWOOD
  Anonymous
  Source Unknown

THAT BASIC TRUTH
  Ralph W. Sockman
  Source Unknown

FIND YOUR ARTICHOKES
  Anonymous
  Source Unknown

WISDOM OR A GOAT
Anonymous
Source Unknown

PURPOSE OF LIFE
Anonymous
Source Unknown

BELIEVE WITHOUT UNDERSTANDING
Anonymous
Source Unknown

TEST IN HONESTY
Anonymous
Source Unknown

JOSH AND HIS JAG
Josh Ridker
Personal Conversation

THE DISMISSAL RITE
Mark Link, S.J.
Illustrated Sunday Homilies, 1990, p. 36

LIVE MORE ABUNDANTLY (ADAPTED)
William Arthur Ward
Used with permission

MORE THAN HOLY WORDS
Anonymous
Source Unknown

PEOPLE WHO KEEP THE WORLD RUNNING
Anonymous
Source Unknown

LIFE IS AN EMPTY BOTTLE
  Anonymous
  Source Unknown

THE GREAT GUEST IN RHYME
  Anonymous
  Source Unknown

YOU HAVE A SPECIAL MESSAGE TO DELIVER
  Anonymous
  Source Unknown

ON THE WINGS OF SUCCESS OR FAILURE
  Anonymous
  Source Unknown

ON THE WRONG TRAIN
  Warren Wiersbe
  Good News Broadcasting, 1988

TWO GOLDEN DAYS
  Robert J. Burdette
  Source Unknown

WHAT'S EATING YOU?
  Lewis Thomas
  Source Unknown

"LOAFS" AND FISHES
  Anonymous
  Source Unknown

GLOOMY GUS
  W.A.M. Stover
  How To Find Inner Peace & Learn To Relax
  NY: Hawthorn Books, 1973

RATING CODE FOR SERMONS
Anonymous
Religious News Service

SUPERMARKET SWEEPSTAKES
Anonymous
Source Unknown

A PENANCE TO REMEMBER
Ronald Mohnickey, T.O.R.
Used with permission

A ROYAL DECREE
Anonymous
Source Unknown

MORE TO LIFE
Grant Teaff
Source Unknown

HAPPINESS WILL FOLLOW
Anonymous
Source Unknown

THE HUMBLE THORNBUSH
Anonymous
Source Unknown

THE STATION
Robert J. Hastings
Source Unknown

THE ISLAND SHELL (ADAPTED)
Anne Morrow Lindbergh
Gift from the Sea
NY: Vintage Books, 1978, pp. 58–59

THE POWER TO CHANGE
    Dr. Maxwell Maltz
    Psycho-Cybernetics
    NY: Pocket Books, 1972, p. 48

IF YOU WON'T, WHO WILL?
    The Christophers
    What a Day This Can Be!

THE SERVANT OF THE KINGDOM
    French Fable
    Source Unknown

INVENTIVE SUCCESS
    Thomas Alva Edison
    Source Unknown

THE UNBREAKABLE CHAIN
    Anonymous
    Source Unknown

THE BEAUTIFUL AND MYSTICAL RIVER
(ADAPTED)
    Kenneth J. Willers
    Celebration, October 1990
    Used with permission

MAINTAIN INTEGRITY
    Anonymous
    Source Unknown

YOU KNEW WHAT I WAS
    Iron Eyes Cody
    Source Unknown

THE HARNESS-MAKER'S SON
   Anonymous
   Source Unknown

FOR THE LOVE OF ...
   Anonymous
   Source Unknown

FAITH IN ABILITY
   Anonymous
   Source Unknown

WHERE DO MERMAIDS STAND? (ADAPTED)
   attributed to Robert Fulghum by Mrs. Barbara Bush
   during Commencement address at Wellesley College,
   June 1, 1990
   Source Unknown

THE BAG AIN'T FULL YET
   William Arthur Ward
   Used with permission

STRENGTH THROUGH STRUGGLE
   Dr. Myrle Swicegood
   Think & Grow Rich, August 1990
   Used with permission

TWO BUCKETS AT THE WELL
   Anonymous
   Source Unknown

THE STAR
   Anonymous
   Source Unknown

THE CHRISTMAS SHELL (ADAPTED)
Gerald Horton Bath
Source Unknown

THE VILLAGE STORYTELLER
Anonymous
Source Unknown

TRUE REFORM
Anonymous
Source Unknown

FILL THE TANK FIRST
Dr. E. Stanley Jones
Source Unknown

FORGIVENESS BEGINS NEW LIFE
Doris Donnelly
Source Unknown

THE ROOT SYSTEM IS TRUST
Elaine M. Prevallet, S.L.
Weavings, September–October, 1990, p. 17
1908 Grand Avenue, PO Box 189, Nashville, TN
37202
Used with permission of the author

TWO PATHS OF LIFE
Anonymous
Source Unknown

WAR OR PEACE
Anonymous
Source Unknown

WINGS OF A DREAM
   Anonymous
   Source Unknown

ON READING THE BIBLE
   Anonymous
   Source Unknown

WHERE'S HEADQUARTERS?
   Anonymous
   Source Unknown

MOSES AND BUSH
   The Joyful Noiseletter, Vol. 5, #9, p. 2
   Fellowship of Merry Christians
   PO Box 895, Portage, MI 49081
   Reprinted with permission

ARE THERE LAWYERS IN HEAVEN?
   Msgr. Arthur Tonne
   Jokes Priests Can Tell, Vol. 7

DO YOU KNOW WHO I AM?
   Anonymous
   Source Unknown

FACING RIVERS OF DIFFICULTIES
   Herb Smith
   Pulpit Helps, November 1990, p. 20
   PO Box 22000, Chattanooga, TN 37422–2000
   Used with permission

FULL-TIME OCCUPATION
   Anonymous
   Source Unknown

GOOD—BETTER—BEST
   Brian Cavanaugh, T.O.R.
   Personal Reflection

DREAMS TO BUILD ON
   Anonymous
   Source Unknown

OUT OF THE PIT
   Anonymous
   Source Unknown

HOW TO RAISE A DELINQUENT
   J. Edgar Hoover
   Source Unknown

CONFIDENCE AND TEAMWORK
   Anonymous
   Source Unknown

A GRANDFATHER'S PRAYER
   Barry Lopez
   Source Unknown

GABRIEL'S SECRET FEAR
   Frederick Buechner
   Peculiar Treasures
   NY: Harper & Row, 1979

CHRISTMAS COOKIES
   Pat Stackhouse
   A Book of Christmas
   Nashville, TN: Upper Room, 1988, p. 53
   Used with permission of the author

SUCCESS THROUGH ADVERSITY
Anonymous
Think & Grow Rich, January 1991, p. 4
Used with permission

IN GOD'S TIME
Anonymous
Source Unknown

Storytelling Reading List

A Book of Christmas: Readings for Reflection during Advent and Christmas. Nashville: The Upper Room, 1988.

Abrahams, Roger D., ed. *African Folktales: Traditional Stories of the Black World.* New York: Pantheon Books–Random House, 1983.

Aesop's Fables. London: Bracken Books, 1986.

Afasas'ev, Aleksandr, ed. *Russian Fairy Tales.* New York: Pantheon Books–Random House, 1983.

Allison, Christine, ed. *Teach Your Children Well.* New York: Bantam–Delacorte Press, 1993.

Applebaum, Rabbi Morton and Rabbi Samuel M. Silver, eds. *Speak to the Children of Israel.* KTAV Publishing House, Inc., 1976.

Arcodia, Charles. *Stories for Sharing.* Newtown, Australia: E.J. Dwyer, Ltd., 1991.

Aurelio, John. *Story Sunday.* Mahwah: Paulist Press, 1978.

———. *Fables for God's People.* New York: Crossroad, 1988.

———. *Colors! Stories of the Kingdom.* New York: Crossroad, 1993.

Ausubel, Nathan, ed. *A Treasury of Jewish Folklore.* New York: Crown Publishers, 1948.

Barker, Esther T. *The Unused Cradle.* Nashville: The Upper Room, 1968.

Bausch, William. *Storytelling: Imagination and Faith.* Mystic: Twenty-Third Publications, 1984.

Bell, Martin. *The Way of the Wolf: Stories, Poems, Songs and Thoughts on the Parables of Jesus.* New York: Ballantine Books/Epiphany Edition, 1983.

Benjamin, Don-Paul, Ron Miner. *Come Sit With Me Again:*

Sermons for Children. New York: The Pilgrim Press, 1987.

Bennett, William J., ed. *The Book of Virtues: A Treasury of Great Moral Stories.* New York: Simon & Schuster, 1993.

Bettelheim, Bruno. *The Uses of Enchantment.* New York: Vintage Books, 1977.

Bodo, O.F.M., Murray. *Tales of St. Francis: Ancient Stories for Contemporary Living.* New York: Doubleday, 1988.

Boyer, Mark. *Following the Star: Daily Reflections for Advent and Christmas.* Liguori: Liguori Publications, 1989.

Briggs, Katharine. *An Encyclopedia of Fairies.* New York: Pantheon Books–Random House, 1976.

Bruchac, Joseph and Michael J. Caduto. *Native American Stories.* Golden: Fulcrum Publishing, 1991.

Brunvand, Jan Harold. *Curses! Broiled Again!* New York: W.W. Norton & Co., 1989.

Buber, Martin. *Tales of the Hasidim: Early Masters.* New York: Schocken Books, 1975.

––––––. *Tales of the Hasidim: Later Masters.* New York: Schocken Books, 1948.

Bushnaq, Inea, ed. *Arab Folktales.* New York: Pantheon Books–Random House, 1986.

Byrd, Charles W. *The Fall of the Sparrow.* Lima: C.S.S. Publishing Company, Inc., 1990.

Calvino, Italo, ed. *Italian Folktales.* New York: Pantheon Books–Random House, 1980.

Carroll, James. *Wonder and Worship.* New York: Newman Press, 1970.

Cassady, Marsh. *Storytelling: Step by Step.* San Jose: Resource Publications, 1990.

Castagnola, S.J., Larry. *More Parables for Little People.* San Jose: Resource Publications, Inc, 1987.

Cattan, Henry. *The Garden of Joys: An Anthology of Oriental Anecdotes, Fables and Proverbs.* London: Namara Publications, Ltd., 1979.

Cavanaugh, Brian, T.O.R. *The Sower's Seeds: One Hundred*

Inspiring Stories for Preaching, Teaching and Public Speaking. Mahwah: Paulist Press, 1990.

———. *More Sower's Seeds: Second Planting.* Mahwah: Paulist Press, 1992.

———. *Fresh Packet of Sower's Seeds: Third Planting.* Mahwah: Paulist Press, 1994.

Chalk, Gary. *Tales of Ancient China.* London: Frederick Muller, 1984.

Chappell, Stephen, O.S.B. *Dragons & Demons, Angels & Eagles: Morality Tales for Teens.* St. Louis: Liguori Publications, 1990.

Charlton, James and Barbara Gilson, eds. *A Christmas Treasury of Yuletide Stories & Poems.* New York: Galahad Books–LDAP, 1992.

Chinnen, Allan B., M.D. *Once Upon a Midlife.* New York: Jeremy P. Tarcher–Putnam Book, 1992.

Colaianni, James F., Sr., ed. *Sunday Sermons Treasury of Illustrations.* Pleasantville: Voicings Publications, 1982.

Colaianni, James F., Jr., ed. *Contemportary Sermon Illustrations.* Ventor: Italicus, Inc., 1991.

Colum, Padraic, ed. *A Treasury of Irish Folklore.* 2nd ed. New York: Crown Publishers, Inc., 1967.

Complete Grimm's Fairy Tales, The. New York: Pantheon Books, 1972.

Cornils, Stanley, ed. *34 Two-Minute Talks for Youth and Adults.* Cincinnati: Standard Publications, 1985.

Curtin, Jeremiah, ed. *Myths and Folk Tales of Ireland.* New York: Dover, 1975.

Dasent, George Webbe, ed. *East O' the Sun & West O' the Moon.* New York: Dover, 1970.

De La Fontaine, Jean, ed. *Selected Fables.* New York: Dover, 1968.

de Mello, Anthony, S.J. *The Song of the Bird.* India: Gujarat Sahitya Prakash, 1982.

———. *One Minute Wisdom.* New York: Doubleday & Co, 1986.

———. *Taking Flight.* New York: Doubleday, 1988.

———. *The Heart of the Enlightened*. New York: Doubleday, 1989.

———. *One Minute Nonsense*. Chicago: Loyola University Press, 1992.

———. *More One Minute Nonsense*. Chicago: Loyola University Press, 1993.

Doleski, Teddi. *The Hurt*. Mahwah: Paulist Press, 1983.

———. *Silvester and the Oogaloo Boogaloo*. Mahwah: Paulist Press, 1990.

Erdoes, Richard and Alfonso Ortiz, eds. *American Indian Myths and Legends*. New York: Pantheon Books–Random House, 1984.

Evans, Ivor, ed. *Brewer's Dictionary of Phrase & Fable*. 14th ed. New York: Harper & Row, 1989.

Fahy, Mary. *The Tree That Survived the Winter*. Mahwah: Paulist Press, 1989.

Farra, Harry. *The Little Monk*. Mahwah: Paulist Press, 1994.

Feehan, James A. *Story Power!: Compelling Illustrations for Preaching and Teaching*. Originally published as *Stories for Preachers*. Dublin: Mercier Press, 1988. San Jose: Resource Publications, 1994.

Field, Claud, trans. *Jewish Legends of the Middle Ages*. London: Shapiro Vallentine & Co.

Frankel, Ellen. *The Classic Tales: 4,000 Years of Jewish Lore*. Northvale: Jason Aronson, 1989.

Giono, Jean. *The Man Who Planted Trees*. Vermont: Chelsea Green Publishing Co., 1985.

Girzone, Joseph. *Joshua: A Parable for Today*. New York: Macmillan, 1983.

———. *Joshua and the Children*. New York: Macmillan, 1989.

Glassie, Henry, ed. *Irish Folk Tales*. New York: Pantheon Books–Random House, 1985.

Graves, Alfred. *The Irish Fairy Book*. New York: Greenwich House, 1983.

Hasler, Richard A. *God's Game Plan: Sports Anecdotes for Preachers*. Lima: C.S.S. Publishing Company, Inc., 1990.

Haugaard, Erik Christian, trans. *Hans Christian Anderson:*

The Complete Fairy Tales and Stories. New York: Anchor–Doubleday, 1974.

Haviland, Virginia, ed. *North American Legends*. New York: Philomel Books, 1979.

Hays, Edward. *Twelve and One-Half Keys*. Leavenworth: Forest of Peace Books, 1981.

———. *Sundancer: A Mystical Fantasy*. Leavenworth: Forest of Peace Books, 1982.

———. *The Ethiopian Tattoo Shop*. Leavenworth: Forest of Peace Books, 1983.

———. *St. George and the Dragon and the Quest for the Holy Grail*. Leavenworth: Forest of Peace Books, 1986.

———. *A Pilgrim's Almanac: Reflections for Each Day of the Year*. Leavenworth: Forest of Peace Books, Inc., 1989.

———. *In Pursuit of the Great White Rabbit: Reflections on a Practical Spirituality*. Leavenworth: Forest of Peace Books, 1990.

———. *The Magic Lantern*. Leavenworth: Forest of Peace Books, 1991.

———. *The Christmas Eve Storyteller*. Leavenworth: Forest of Peace Books, 1992.

———. *Holy Fools & Mad Hatters*. Leavenworth: Forest of Peace Books, 1993.

———. *The Quest for the Flaming Pearl*. Leavenworth: Forest of Peace Books, 1994.

Henderschedt, James L. *The Magic Stone*. San Jose: Resource Publications, Inc. (160 E. Virginia Street, S-290), 1988.

———. *The Topsy-Turvy Kingdom*. San Jose: Resource Publications, Inc. (160 E. Virginia Street, S-290), 1990.

———. *The Light in the Lantern*. San Jose: Resource Publications, Inc. (160 E. Virginia Street, S-290), 1991.

Holdcraft, Paul E., ed. *Snappy Stories for Sermons and Speeches*. Nashville: Abingdon Press, 1987.

Holt, David and Bill Mooney. *Ready-to-Tell Tales*. Little Rock: August House, 1994.

Hunt, Angela Elwell. *The Tale of Three Trees: A Traditional*

Folktale. Batavia: Lion Publishing Corp., 1989 (1705 Hubbard Ave., Batavia, IL 60510).

Jaffe, Nina and Steve Zeitlin, eds. *While Standing on One Foot: Puzzle Stories and Wisdom Tales from the Jewish Tradition.* New York: Henry Holt, 1993.

Johnson, Miriam. *Inside Twenty-Five Classic Children's Stories.* Mahwah: Paulist Press, 1986.

Juknialis, Joseph. *Winter Dreams and Other Such Friendly Dragons.* San Jose: Resource Publications, Inc, 1979.

Killinger, John. *Parables for Christmas.* Nashville: Abingdon Press, 1985.

———. *Christmas Spoken Here.* Nashville: Broadman Press, 1989.

Kronberg, Ruthilde and Patricia C. McKissack. *A Piece of the Wind and Other Stories To Tell.* New York: Harper & Row, 1990.

Kurtz, Ernest and Katherine Ketchman. *The Spirituality of Imperfection: Storytelling and the Journey to Wholeness.* New York: Bantam, 1992.

Lang, Andrew, ed. *The Brown Fairy Book.* New York: Dover, 1965.

L'Estrange, Sir Rodger. *Fables of Aesop.* Drawings by Alexander Calder. New York: Dover Publications, 1967.

Levin, Meyer. *Classic Hasidic Tales.* New York: Dorset Press, 1985.

Levine, David, ed. *The Fables of Aesop.* New York: Dorset Press, 1989.

Lewis, Naomi, ed. *Cry Wolf and Other Aesop Fables.* New York: Oxford University Press, 1988.

Lieberman, Leo and Arthur Beringause. *Classics of Jewish Literature.* Secaucus: Book Sales, Inc., 1988.

Livo, Norma J. and Sandra A. Rietz. *Storytelling: Process & Practice.* Littleton: Libraries Unlimited, Inc., 1986.

———. *Storytelling Folklore Sourcebook.* Littleton: Libraries Unlimited, Inc., 1991.

Lobel, Arnold. *Fables.* New York: Harper Collins, 1980.

Loder, Ted. *Tracks in the Snow: Tales Spun from the Manger.* San Diego: LuraMedia, 1985.

Lufburrow, Bill. *Illustrations Without Sermons.* Nashville: Abingdon Press, 1985.

Magic Ox and Other Tales of the Effendi, The. Beijing: Foreign Languages Press, 1986.

Marbach, Ethel. *The White Rabbit: A Franciscan Christmas Story.* Cincinnati: St. Anthony Messenger Press, 1984.

Martin, Rafe, ed. *The Hungry Tigress: Buddhist Legends & Jataka Tales.* Berkeley: Parallax Press, 1990.

McArdle, Jack. *150 Stories for Preachers and Teachers.* Mystic: Twenty-Third Publications, 1990.

McCarthy, Flor, S.D.B. *And the Master Answered . . .* Notre Dame: Ave Maria Press, 1985.

Mellon, Nancy. *Storytelling & the Art of Imagination.* Rockport: Element, Inc., 1992.

Meyer, Gabriel. *In the Shade of the Terebinth: Tales of a Night Journey.* Leavenworth: Forest of Peace Publishing, 1994.

Miller, Donald. *The Gospel and Mother Goose.* Elgin: Brethren Press, 1987.

Minghella, Anthony, ed. *Jim Henson's The Storyteller.* New York: Borzoi–Alfred A. Knopf, Inc., 1991.

National Storytelling Association, The. *Tales as Tools: The Power of Story in the Classroom.* Jonesborough: The National Storytelling Press, 1994.

————. *Storytelling* magazine. NSA, PO Box 309, Jonesborough, TN 37659.

Newcombe, Jack. *A Christmas Treasury.* New York: Viking Press, 1982.

Night the Stars Sang, The: The Wonder That Is Christmas. Tarrytown: Gleneida Publishing Group–Triumph Books, 1991 (by special arrangement with Guidepost Books).

Nomura, Yushi. *Desert Wisdom: Sayings From the Desert Fathers.* New York: Image Books, 1984.

O'Connor, Ulick. *Irish Tales & Sagas.* London: Dragon Books, 1985.

O'Faolain, Eileen. *Irish Sagas and Folk Tales*. New York: Avenel Books, 1982.

Olszewski, Daryl. *Balloons! Candy! Toys! and Other Parables for Storytellers*. San Jose: Resource Publications, 1986.

Parry-Jones, D., ed. *Welsh Legends & Fairy Lore*. New York: Barnes & Noble–Marboro Books by arrangement with B.T. Batsford, Ltd., 1992.

Paulus, Trina. *Hope for the Flowers*. Mahwah: Paulist Press, 1972.

Pellowski, Anne. *The World of Storytelling*. Revised edition. New York: H.W. Wilson, 1990.

Pennel, Jr., Joe E. *The Whisper of Christmas: Reflections for Advent and Christmas*. Nashville: The Upper Room, 1984.

Polsky, Howard W. and Yaella Wozner. *Everyday Miracles: The Healing Wisdom of Hasidic Stories*. Northvale: Jason Aronson Inc., 1989.

Powers, C.P., Isaias. *Nameless Faces in the Life of Jesus*. Mystic: Twenty-Third Publications, 1981.

———. *Father Ike's Stories for Children*. Mystic: Twenty-Third Publications, 1988.

Prather, Hugh and Gayle Prather. *Parables from Other Planets*. New York: Bantam Books, 1991.

Ramanujan, A.K., ed. *Folktales from India*. New York: Pantheon Books–Random House, 1991.

Reynolds, David K., Ph.D. *Playing Ball on Running Water*. New York: Quill, 1984.

———. *Even in Summers the Ice Doesn't Melt*. New York: Quill, 1986.

———. *Water Bears No Scars*. New York: Quill, 1987.

———. *Pools of Lodging for the Moon: Strategy for a Positive Life-Style*. New York: William Morrow & Co., 1989.

———. *A Thousand Waves: A Sensible Life-Style for Sensitive People*. New York: William Morrow & Co., 1990.

Robbennolt, Roger. *Tales of Tonny Great Turtle*. Leavenworth: Forest of Peace Publishing, 1994.

Seuss, Dr. *Oh, the Places You'll Go!* New York: Random House, 1990.

Shea, John. *The Spirit Master.* Chicago: Thomas More Press, 1987.

———. *Starlight: Beholding the Christmas Miracle All Year Long.* New York: Crossroad Publishing, 1992.

Simpkinson, Charles & Anne Simpkinson, eds. *Sacred Stories: A Celebration of the Power of Stories To Transform and Heal.* San Francisco: HarperSanFrancisco, 1993.

Singer, Isaac Bashevis. *Stories for Children.* New York: Farrar, Straus, Giroux, 1984.

———. *The Image and Other Stories.* London: Jonathan Cape, Ltd., 1985.

Smith, Richard Gordon. *Ancient Tales and Folklore of Japan.* London: Bracken Books, 1986.

Stanton, Sue. *Boston and the Feast of St. Francis.* Mahwah: Paulist Press, 1994.

Stoddard, Sandol. *The Rules and Mysteries of Brother Solomon.* Mahwah: Paulist Press, 1987.

Stromberg, Bob. *Why Geese Fly Farther Than Eagles.* Colorado Springs: Focus on the Family Publ., 1992.

Sutherland, Zena and Myra Cohn Livingston, eds. *The Scott, Foresman Anthology of Children's Literature.* Chicago: Scott, Foresman and Co., 1984.

Tazewell, Charles. *The Littlest Angel.* Nashville: Ideals Publishing, 1946.

Thoma, Clemens and Michael Wyschogrod, eds. *Parable and Story in Judaism and Christianity.* Mahwah: Paulist Press, 1989.

Thompson, Stith. *The Folktale.* Los Angeles: The University of California Press, 1977.

Valles, Carlos G., S.J. *Tales of the City of God.* Chicago: Loyola University Press, 1993.

Vecsey, Christopher. *Imagine Ourselves Richly: Mythic Narratives of North American Indians.* San Francisco: HarperCollins, 1991.

Weinreich, Beatrice Silverman, ed. *Yiddish Folktales.* Translated by Leonard Wolf. New York: Pantheon–Random House, 1988.

Wharton, Paul, ed. *Stories and Parables for Preachers and Teachers*. Mahwah: Paulist Press, 1986.

White, William R., ed. *Speaking in Stories*. Minneapolis: Augsburg, 1982.

———. *Stories for Telling*. Minneapolis: Augsburg, 1986.

———. *Stories for the Journey*. Minneapolis: Augsburg, 1988.

Wiesel, Elie. *Souls on Fire: Portraits and Legends of Hasidic Masters*. New York: Summit Books, 1972.

———. *Somewhere a Master: Further Hasidic Portraits and Legends*. New York: Summit Books, 1981.

Wilde, Oscar. *The Happy Prince and Other Fairy Tales*. New York: Dover, 1992.

———. *The Fairy Tales of Oscar Wilde*. New York: Henry Holt & Co., 1993.

Wood, Douglas. *Old Turtle*. Duluth: Pfeifer-Hamilton Publishers, 1992.

Yolen, Jane, ed. *Favorite Folktales from Around the World*. New York: Pantheon Books–Random House, 1986.

Zipes, Jack, ed. *Spells of Enchantment: The Wondrous Fairy Tales of Western Culture*. New York: Viking–Penguin, 1991.

———. *Aesop's Fables . . . and 200 Other Famous Fables*. New York: Signet Classic-Penguin, 1992.

Theme Index

Theme:	Story Numbers:
Education	34, 35, 59, 60, 91
Emmaus	37
Encouragement	5, 21, 22, 38, 95
Entrepreneur	5, 92, 99
Epiphany	6
Ethics	26, 65
Eucharist	37, 48
Evangelization	6, 16, 27, 37
Evil	77, 88
Excellence	21, 91
Experience	64, 66, 72
Faith	7, 20, 27, 34, 54, 64, 74, 75, 89, 97
Family	2, 9, 10, 12, 22, 53, 68, 74, 79, 80, 88, 94, 96
Fear	18, 33, 38, 46, 54, 57, 80, 89
Forgiveness	9, 79, 98
Fund Raising	100
Gifts/Talents	43, 60, 71, 95
Goals	15, 21, 62
God's Will	54, 97
Golden Rule	10, 25, 33
Good Deeds	24, 93
Good Friday	29, 56
Gospel Witness	7, 10, 27, 37, 51, 74, 84, 90
Graduation	51, 70
Gratitude	27, 54, 75
Greed	24, 51
Happiness	55, 57, 71, 73, 88
Healing	36, 47, 79
Hell	24, 61, 87
Holiness	39, 68
Holy Week	2, 29, 56

Theme:	Story Numbers:
Honesty	35, 65
Hope	46, 59, 83
Hospitality	42, 53
Humility	18, 56, 86
Humor	11, 12, 13, 17, 32, 45, 48, 49, 50, 52, 55, 61, 85, 86, 87, 93, 100
Incarnation	42, 97
Integrity	26, 33, 35, 65
Jesus Christ	42, 64, 68
Joy	64, 75
Leadership	21, 85, 95
Lent	9, 20, 27, 28, 29, 33, 36, 38, 68, 93
Life, Meaning of	13, 33, 43, 45, 55, 74
Life's Journey	46, 51, 57, 62, 64, 72, 77, 81, 89, 91
Limitations	38, 59
Lincoln, Abe	85
Liturgy	37
Love	2, 4, 13, 22, 41, 68, 79
Management	21, 85, 95
Marriage	27, 88
Medicine	2, 41
Michelangelo	69
Mid-Life	26, 38, 61
Ministry	42, 61
Mission	6, 37, 43, 75, 93
Motivation	3, 5, 21
Nature	29, 30, 31, 34, 38, 47, 80
Noah's Ark	17
Opportunity	3, 67
Parents	45, 59, 72, 94
Peace	77, 82
Penance	20, 52

Theme:	Story Numbers:
Perseverance	28, 44, 62, 92, 99
Politics	32, 61, 77, 86
Prayer	4, 11, 24, 39, 54, 58, 78, 96
Preaching	7, 16, 50
Preparation	19, 42, 78
Pride	15, 21
Problem Solving	62, 99
Public Office	61
Racism	70
Reconciliation	9, 18, 27, 98
Redemption	68
Regret	46, 57
Relationships	53, 76, 79, 80, 88
Religious Life	39
Repentance	11, 12, 20, 63
Resentment	49
Respect	5, 22, 70
Responsibility	25, 63, 77, 94
Reverence	96
Sacraments	80
Sacred Heart	8, 68
Sacrifice	2, 75
Saints	60, 64
Salvation	24, 51
Self-Confidence	59, 64, 69
Self-Esteem	5, 49
Selfishness	2, 24, 25
Sermon on the Mount	4
Service	40, 61
Sin	24, 63, 66
Sorrow	88
Sow/Reap	22, 23, 24, 71
Spiritual Direction	45
Spirituality	39, 64, 66, 80, 84

Theme:	Story Numbers:
Sports	14, 17, 18, 21, 54, 65, 95
Spring Break	13
St. Francis of Assisi	77
St. Joseph	40
Students	15, 60
Success	15, 19, 44, 57, 62, 64, 65, 99
Teaching	15, 59, 60, 72
Teenagers	66, 91, 94
Temptation	4, 66
Thanksgiving	54
Today	3, 46
Transformation	5, 26
Truman, Harry	82
Trust	80, 97
Understanding	1, 34, 43
Values	22, 35
Virgin Mary	97
Vocation	43, 90
War	82
Wilson, Woodrow	83
Wisdom	1, 32, 33, 55, 66
Worry	3, 18, 46, 47
Youth	13, 27, 32